# THE ANCIENT PERSIANS
## HOW THEY LIVED AND WORKED

# The Ancient Persians

## HOW THEY LIVED AND WORKED

Brian Dicks

DAVID & CHARLES

NEWTON ABBOT   LONDON   NORTH POMFRET (Vt)

This book is dedicated to the secretarial, cartographic and photographic personnel of the Geography Department of the University of Strathclyde, Glasgow.

**British Library Cataloguing in Publication Data**

Dicks, Brian
The Ancient Persians, how they lived and worked.
(How they lived and worked).
1. Iran Social life and customs  2. Iran – History
To 640
I. Title  II. Series
935          DS267
ISBN –0–7153–7711–6

Photoset and printed in Great Britain by
REDWOOD BURN LIMITED  TROWBRIDGE & ESHER
for David & Charles (Publishers) Limited
Brunel House  Newton Abbot  Devon

Published in the United States of America
by David & Charles Inc
North Pomfret  Vermont 05053  USA

# Contents

# List of Illustrations

Then there will appear a warrior king. He will rule a vast kingdom and will do what he chooses.

*Daniel* xi, 3

# *I*

# *The Search for the Persians*

THE rise of the Persian empire has been regarded as one of the most momentous events in the history of the ancient world. In little more than a generation, beginning somewhere around 560 BC, an obscure tribal family of Asiatic origin became the creators of the first great universal empire of recorded history, one which incorporated vaster lands, more numerous peoples and more diverse cultures than its predecessors of Babylon, Egypt and Assyria. What had been, for 3,000 years, a gateway and land of transit where armies, merchandise and ideas had entered the Middle East now became the centre of gravity of the first commonwealth of nations in which the king was the symbol of its unity as well as the source of its power. Persian hegemony, under the Achaemenian ruling house, reached its zenith with Darius the Great (522–486 BC), when the empire extended over a territory of nearly 2 million square miles (5 million sq km) and housed a population estimated at around 10 million.

The 2,500th anniversary of the founding of the Persian empire by Cyrus the Great was celebrated in 1971. In a lavish tented city, situated below the 33 acre (13.3ha) platform which supports the ruins of Persepolis (the Achaemenian dynastic and ceremonial capital), the modern sovereign, Mohammed Reza Shah Pahlevi, played host to nearly half the world's monarchs and heads of state. The dignitaries were housed in luxury tents laid out around a magnificent fountain, and the tented apartments of the Shah and Empress Farah were lined with

9

purple velvet curtains and specially woven purple carpets. In the dining area the guests sat on blue velvet-covered chairs of French manufacture and a French firm also produced the 190ft (58m) long hand-embroidered tablecloth.

These anniversary celebrations echoed the pomp, opulence and luxury of the palaces and courts of the ancient Persian empire. The fact that they took place at Persepolis, rather than Pasargadae, the city founded by Cyrus the Great, was reminiscent of the ancient Persian custom at Nawruz, or New Year, when the Achaemenian kinship was renewed and the lords and vassals pitched their tents in the plain around Persepolis as part of the preparations for the solemn homage procession before the King of Kings. These colourful and impressive scenes are depicted in the realistic bas-reliefs at Persepolis where representatives of the subject nations, from the Greek islands to India and from Central Asia to Ethiopia, brought their exotic gifts to the Persian rulers. The homage parade was followed by a sumptuous feast and in a second ceremony the king, seated on a high throne, was carried by the dignitaries of the conquered nations.

Though television carried pictures of the Shah's celebrations throughout the world, few people were aware of his country's origins and little was known of its early rulers. The story of ancient Persia has always been a subject of speculation and less than a generation ago it was nothing more than a confused patchwork of myth and legend. The Old Testament accounts in the Book of Esther of the richness and intrigue in the court of Ahasuerus (Xerxes) and proverbial references to the 'law of the Medes and Persians which altereth not' (Daniel vi, 12) were regarded as little more than fable or symbolism, as were the writings of the Greeks, particularly Herodotus. Thus Persia appeared to have emerged into the limelight of the ancient world almost overnight, fully fledged and powerful enough to take a major lead in world affairs.

Gradually, though still incompletely, an authentic historical record of the ancient Persian empire is taking shape and a remarkable picture of human achievement is now emerging. This is largely the result of archaeological exploration and research which have either refuted or corroborated earlier ideas based on classical writings and isolated discoveries. With the exception of a number of trilingual inscriptions (attributable mainly to Darius and Xerxes), and the religious book the *Avesta*, the Persians failed to write their own history. There are no great archival treasure-houses—as with the Egyptians and Hittites—to provide information on national customs and events, or insights into the personalities and domestic activities of kings and subjects. While some Assyrian, Egyptian and Babylonian chronicles contain passing references to the Persians, the major written sources are the Greek writers, chiefly Herodotus but also Thucydides, Xenophon and Ctesias.

Though the Greeks provide the only real contemporary accounts of the ancient Persians, they had little reason to be sympathetic or impartial to an empire that had engulfed the Greek colonies of Asia Minor and had repeatedly attacked the Greek mainland. Their stories were told in terms of protracted wars and spectacular naval battles, usually written from the Greek point of view and implying the gallant defence of western culture against oriental despotism. The theme of Aeschylus' *The Persians*, based on the author's personal experiences of the battle of Marathon (490 BC), is that of a free nation making its stand against aggression. Though critical, the Greeks respected the Persians, and the writings of Herodotus and Xenophon in particular are full of admiration for their achievement. Xenophon's *Cyropaedia* is an idealised account of the education of Cyrus the Great whom the Greeks looked upon as a model ruler. Xenophon also produced the *Anabasis*, or *Persian Expedition*, describing his adventures with the 10,000 mercenaries enlisted by Cyrus the Younger against his brother and rival Artaxerxes II.

Herodotus' *History of the Greek and Persian War* is the standard contemporary work on the Persian empire, though many sections of the nine-book account are of doubtful reliability, being based on traditions, myths that grew up around distant events and 'facts' that were handed down over many centuries. From his birthplace at Halicarnassus, near Bodrum in western Asia Minor, Herodotus (c 484–420BC) travelled widely in the eastern Mediterranean and the Middle East, incorporating observations made on his travels into digressions on anthropology, geography, archaeology and, on occasions, plain gossip. It was these colourful episodes, such as the description of the warlike and one-eyed Arimaspi of the Scythian steppes, or the Hyperboreans who lived in perpetual sunshine and plenty, which made his fellow Greeks attack him as 'the father of lies'. Yet Herodotus is also known as 'the father of history', for he was the first to arrange his sources systematically and critically, and the thoroughness of his research has long been admired. Herodotus' lucid style, his freedom from racial prejudice, his appreciation of the vagaries of human nature and his perceptive interest in personalities combine to make him one of the most readable of classical writers.

Though archaeology and its related disciplines provide the main sources for Persian development, scientific excavation came late to Iran. Even the visible ruins of Persepolis and Pasargadae, visited as early as the sixteenth century by western travellers, were not systematically studied until the 1930s. Before that, Iran remained largely closed to foreign explorers, with the exception of the French. As the country was opened up in the decade before World War II, a number of expeditions were attracted to such sites as Hissar in north-east Iran, Cheshmeh Ali near Tehran, and Persepolis. The French continued their researches at Susa, and at Sialk and Giyan on the plateau. The results of this work, though unco-ordinated and hampered by problems of dating and decipherment, enriched beyond measure an understanding of ancient Persia's contribution to civilisation, not least in arts and crafts. The 1950s saw the beginnings of organised research programmes with clearly defined aims. Today, under the auspices and encouragement of the Iranian Archaeological Service, extensive scientific investigation is being undertaken by Britain, the United States, France, Germany, Belgium, Italy, Denmark, Sweden, Japan and Canada.

Though archaeology has transformed our appreciation of Persia's great legacy to the world, many aspects of the empire's lifestyles in peace and in war remain obscure owing to the paucity of records. According to B.N. Frye, in *The Heritage of Persia*, 'we have not even a fragmentary net with great holes in it but merely bits of information which we must try to fit together into some framework'. J. Hicks, in *The Emergence of Man: The Persians*, agrees. 'Despite the techniques of archaeology,' he states, 'little is available today that was not familiar to any intelligent, concerned citizen of ancient Athens who went to the market place to hear read aloud Herodotus' history of the Persian Wars.' These statements may obviously be challenged, but certainly knowledge of the Persian empire is sketchy in detail and subject to question and dispute. Scores of complex problems seek answers, generalisations are unavoidable and inferences and probabilities continue to characterise current writings on the ancient Persians. Their history will no doubt be considerably amplified and clarified if the current rate of research and discovery is maintained. Inevitably this will illuminate further the material culture of what is now acknowledged to have been a vigorous and highly sophisticated society, and one which contributed to civilisation in the broadest sense.

# 2

# The Country and the People

THE terms *Persia* and *Iran* have been used interchangeably to identify the same geographical area. The modern country, covering approximately 636,300 square miles (1,648,000 sq km) is roughly seven times the size of the United Kingdom and six times that of the state of Colorado. Politically it is a descendant of the Persian empire of antiquity, though that encompassed extensive territories to the east and west of the modern boundaries. In a physical sense parts of Russia, Afghanistan, Pakistan and Turkey are a continuation of the Iranian plateau, which traditionally extends from the Mesopotamian lowlands to the Hindu Kush, and from the Persian Gulf and Arabian Sea to the Caspian Sea and the steppes of Turkestan.

*Persia*, a designation first applied by the Greeks, is taken from the south-western part of this plateau region—the province of *Parsa* (*Persis* to the Greeks and subsequently, to the Arabs, *Fars*). Though *Parsa* formed a single province in a great empire it was the homeland of the Achaemenians, the Persian ruling house, and its name was commonly applied by westerners to the whole of the empire. Its inhabitants, however, referred to their land as *Iran* (*Eran*), sometimes *Iranshahr* (the state of Iran) or *Iranzamin* (the land of Iran). These terms derive from *Aryan*, the general and collective name for peoples speaking related Indo-European tongues and dialects who invaded and settled the plateau lands during the second and first millennia BC.

### THE GEOGRAPHICAL BACKGROUND

As the western and larger part of the traditional Iranian plateau, Persia has been likened to a great physiographic bowl, for
basically it consists of a complex of mountain chains encircling
and enclosing an irregular and lower—but not low-lying—
interior (Figure 1). For the most part this interior is a series of
arid basins of some 300,000 square miles (780,000sq km) that lie
at altitudes of 980 to 4,300ft (300 to 1,300m) above sea level. The
largest, separated by an inner mountain chain, are the Dasht-i-
Kavir and the Dasht-i-Lut, which together with similar basins
in Afghanistan and Pakistan (Dasht-i-Margo and Dasht-i-
Tahlab) are reputed to be the most arid areas in the world and
are still largely unexplored. This desert interior has always
acted as a barrier to east-west communications, diverting trade
routes to the north and south and directing migratory peoples
either eastwards to India or westwards to Mesopotamia via the
Caspian and Caucasian routes.

In the west the extensive mountain chains of Kurdistan and
the Zagros separate the interior desert basins from the Tigris-
Euphrates lowlands. These ranges, with altitudes of between
6,500 and 13,100ft (2,000 and 4,000m), extend in a north-west to
south-east direction for over 1,000 miles (1,600km), dominating
the entire western part of Iran. They form a complex of parallel
chains with intervening valleys and intermontane plateaux,
and contain some of the most imposing fold structures and
mountain peaks in the Middle East. From the Mesopotamian
lowlands the Zagros, in particular, forms a defensive bulwark
whose only practicable routes to the plateau are the passes that
connect Kermanshah to Hamadan ('the gateway to Asia') and
the Persian Gulf lowlands, via Shiraz, to ancient Persepolis
('the Persian Gates'). Through the former, the armies of Darius
I marched westwards, and subsequently the armies of Alexander the Great and the Arab conquerors marched eastwards.

Situated on the south-western flanks of the central Zagros,
where the Karun river flows from the mountain ranges to the
Persian Gulf, is the plain of Khuzistan, or ancient Susiana. This

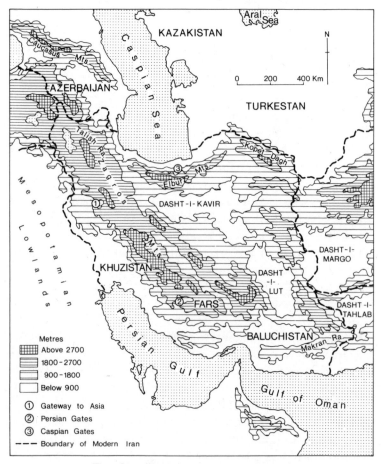

Fig 1   Iran (Persia): generalised relief map

triangular riverine area is an extension of Mesopotamia and the largest single expanse of lowland within Iran's modern boundaries. Here Elam, with its capital at Susa, was the earliest centre of urban civilisation and political organisation in Persia, and Susa was destined to become the chief administrative and communications centre of the Achaemenian empire.

The mountain chains continue to the south-east of

Khuzistan to form the upland province of Fars (Parsa, Persis). A succession of north-west to south-east trending ranges and valleys are separated from the Persian Gulf coast by a narrow and inhospitable coastal strip, traditionally unfavourable to settlement and maritime activity. Thus it was inland Fars that was the homeland of the Achaemenian dynasty, but even here the topography and natural lines of communication dictated that the real heart of Persia lay to the north-west—the area of modern Hamadan—Tehran—Isfahan and its extension to Tabriz in Azerbaijan. Crossed by great trade routes and open to invasion from Turkestan and the Caucasus, this region witnessed Iran's most turbulent history. Characteristically, it was the first area to be settled by the Medes and Persians.

The Elburz mountains bound the interior desert basins on the north. They are a continuation of the western Talish range and in the east merge with the Kopet Dagh. The Elburz circumvent the southern shores of the Caspian Sea whose coast rises precipitously from below sea level to a maximum height of 18,550ft (5,654m) in Mount Damavand. Southwards the interior plateau reduces this relative difference in altitude, but the Elburz still provide steep, abrupt slopes which act as formidable defences. The range is vulnerable to the north-east of Tehran where the 'Caspian Gates', below Mount Damavand, link the plateau with the south-east corner of the Caspian and, hence, the Turkestan steppes.

The Kopet Dagh range is continued southwards by mountain complexes which separate Iran from Afghanistan. In the south the circuit is completed by the ranges of Makran, Sistan and Baluchistan. Topographical continuity is broken by a pass which leads from the eastern plateau to Bandar Abbas, formerly a prosperous port at the junction of the Persian Gulf with the Arabian Sea.

## THE PERSONALITY OF IRAN

Within this broad geographical framework Iran's chief areas of early settlement were peripheral to the highland belts proper, that is, those rain-fed areas and oases encircling the plateau which were suitable for cultivation and pastoral pursuits. Geography has dictated that the dominant characteristic of Iran's organised and settled life is its isolated character; from this the fierce individuality of the Persians and their general lack of unity, except under powerful leadership, takes root. Iran's restrictive physical environment has always presented its inhabitants with problems and challenges, and the traditional responses have been the development, almost side by side, of nomadic, semi-nomadic and sedentary ways of life. Throughout history the country has been dominated by the disparity between the shifting habitat of the former and the permanent settlements of the latter. For the Mesopotamian states the civilised and cultured world ended at the Zagros foothills, though there were times, especially under the rule of new and vigorous dynasties, when the pressure of the plain on the mountain and plateau zones was intensified. Conversely the decadence of the riverine civilisations acted as a clarion call to the hill peoples, who descended to pillage, conquer and even settle for varying lengths of time. This unending strugggle between nomadism and sedentary agriculture, revealed on the local, regional and national scale, characterises the rise of Persia and accounts for the progress and power of its empire.

### EARLY FARMERS

While Africa is commonly accepted as the birthplace of humanity, south-west Asia is regarded as its nursery where, in the social and economic senses, *Homo sapiens* evolved and matured. Stone Age man lived in, and migrated across, south-west Asia for 100,000 years or so, during which time major cultural and technological advances occurred. Chief of these was the transition from the hunting and food-gathering stage of livelihood to an economy based on the domestication of animals and the cultivation of crops, chiefly cereals. The period covered by this so-called Neolithic Revolution amounted to several thousand years, probably beginning around the eighth millennium BC. The main stages in this cultural advancement can be gleaned from a substantial number of sites extending from Palestine to Iran and from Anatolia to Arabia.

Neolithic man continued to inhabit caves and rock shelters, but gradually open sites became more common; a combination of favourable location and human conservatism resulted in many sites being occupied for centuries. In the course of time, accumulating debris, relating to this sequent occupance, formed a mound (*tepe, tal* or *tell*) from which the chronology of human remains can be observed and recorded. Archaeologists have shown, however, that cultural progress was not uniform but related to variations in local environment, contacts with neighbouring peoples, migrations and invasions.

The Zagros region was of major significance in the initial stages of farming, for here, as in other parts of the Middle East, prototypes of the earliest domesticated plants and animals existed in a wild state. On the Iraqi side, sites such as Shanidar, Jarmo and Hassuna reveal, almost without stratigraphical breaks, the evolution of early peasant communities from transient, nomadic settlements to mature agricultural villages with permanent habitations. Similarly, in Iranian Khuzistan and Luristan, excavations at sites such as Ganj Dareh and Tepe Guran indicate the increasing cultivation of wheat and barley, together with the rearing of goats and sheep. A considerable population increase accompanied the mastery of cereal cultivation and husbandry, and around 7,000 BC in Khuzistan, village communities greatly prospered from irrigation systems. Similar trends can be traced in Fars, in north-east Iran, in southern Turkestan and at Sialk, south of modern Tehran.

The artificial mound of Tepe Sialk contains some of the earliest traces of man's occupation of the Iranian plateau. Its site is adjacent to an oasis formed by a perennial spring on the western side of the Dasht-i-Kavir. Sialk's first habitations were primitive huts constructed of wooden branches, but above this basal layer are four building levels with dwellings whose construction evolves from the use of irregular lumps of sun-dried mud to rectangular bricks shaped from moulds. At Sialk sheep, goats—and perhaps cattle—were domesticated, and gazelles and other animals were hunted. Stone hoe blades, querns and mortars attest to the importance of cereal cultivation, and the presence of spindle whorls implies spinning and presumably the weaving of textiles. By the seventh millennium BC, Sialk and other sites were linked by a trade in raw materials and finished products, such as pottery and metalwork. From 7,500 BC obsidian from Turkey and cowrie shells from the Persian Gulf were used in Khuzistan, as was turquoise from north-east Iran, native copper from the plateau and red ochre from Fars and Homruz.

Thus in northern Iran the material progress of early agricultural settlements was closely comparable to those of the Mesopotamian lowlands. The peasant communities of the latter, however, were to form the basis on which literate and urban civilisations were built. The natural heart of the Iranian plateau was desert, and localities favourable to early farmers were not initially suited to the emergence of politically larger units. The most likely Iranian territory from this point of view was the low-lying region between the lower Euphrates and the Zagros foothills (modern Khuzistan) which as a physical extension of Mesopotamia provided the setting for the kingdom of Elam. This, together with its somewhat better-known neighbour Sumer, were the earliest urban states with integrated political authority to develop in Mesopotamia during the fourth millennium BC.

THE KINGDOM OF ELAM

Unlike resource-poor Sumer, which was surrounded by the featureless Mesopotamian floodplains, Elam was partly a hill kingdom rich in raw materials. It supplied the Sumerians with silver, copper, tin, lead, precious gems, horses, timber, obsidian, alabaster, diorite and steatite (soapstone). By the first quarter of the third millennium BC the Elamites had established a dynasty and ruled from Susa, their capital, a wide area of plains (Susiana) together with a section of the Zagros and adjacent plateau. The Zagros were occupied by peoples of similar ethnic origin—Kassites, Lullabi and Guti (Figure 2)—who formed part of the great duel between upland nomads and the sedentary populations of the plains. Collectively the Elamites and the hill peoples were of Asiatic or Zagros origin, belonging neither to the Semitic nor to the Indo-European peoples. Some scholars assign them to a group of peoples speaking Caucasian languages.

Early in pre-history the site of Susa testified both to the natural wealth of the province and to the advantage of its position between the Tigris-Euphrates and the Iranian plateau. Copper and bronze metallurgy became Elamite specialisations; the demand for raw materials, not readily available in the plains, stimulated the development of inner Iran as a mining and distributional centre and as a workshop for the production of goods based on local resources. Recent archaeological findings show that the Elamite realm included territory at least 560 miles (900km) to the east of Susa where a subsidiary, but significant, centre of urban culture was found at Tepe Yahya. This Elamite outpost was located midway between the Tigris-Euphrates and the Indus, 56 miles (90km) north of modern Bandar Abbas on the Persian Gulf. Tepe Yahya and sites such as Tal-i-Iblis, Bampur, Nal, Shahdab and Shahr-i-Sokhta appear to have played key roles in the transmission of urban culture from west to east, substantiating Sir Mortimer Wheeler's view that 'the idea of civilisation' crossed from Mesopotamia to the Indus.

Elam was not the only centralised state to establish itself in the Mesopotamian lowlands and initially it was dominated by the Akkadian kings of Sumer and the Third Dynasty of Ur. Around 2000 BC the Elamites were strong enough to attack and destroy Ur, and for nearly 1,000 years maintained some measure of political independence, though much of their history has yet to be written. The thirteenth century BC marks a great cultural revival under a series of masterful kings, whose buildings and inscriptions at Susa and elsewhere provide some of the best evidence of Elamite civilisation. It was during the reign of Silhac-Inshushinac (1165–1151 BC) that Elam's frontiers were extended east to the Iranian plateau. With the death of Inshushinac, Elam was governed by Nebuchadnezzar I of Babylon. A brief nationalistic revival in the eighth and seventh centuries was followed around 640 BC by Elam's inclusion within the Assyrian empire of Ashurbanipal. From the records of these Assyrian campaigns the names of Iranian peoples—the Medes and Persians—are first heard.

### THE ARYANS

The Persians, and the empire subsequently named after them, have their origin in the great Eurasian *völkerwanderung* (folk migration) of Indo-European tribes which culminated towards the end of the second and the beginning of the first millennium BC. From their original homeland of Transoxiana—the plains of southern Russia to the east and north of the Caspian Sea—these people moved in search of land and plunder, and to escape the attacks of hordes, more powerful than themselves, which pressed on their backs. The original Aryan groups were stockbreeders (oxen, sheep, pigs) though they practised a primitive form of cultivation from temporary settlements. They had domesticated the horse and knew weapons of copper and bronze. A major Aryan contribution lay in the field of language: from what must have been a common tongue the Vedic (Sanskrit) Persian, Greek, Latin, Celtic, Slavonic and Teutonic languages became differentiated. Whereas Sumerian, for example, was an agglutinative language in which meanings were achieved by the complex clustering of units, the Indo-European languages had a clear and logical structure. According to Childe, they possessed 'a rudimentary machinery for building subordinate clauses and for expressing conceptual relationships'.

In its narrowest sense the term 'Aryan' (literally 'noble') is applied to divisions within the Indo-European tribal groups who spoke closely related dialects and probably worshipped common deities. In the course of the second millennium, the first wave of Aryans entered western Asia at about the same time as a related branch moved into north-western India. The multi-pronged western migrations (Figure 2) brought the Achaeans to Greece, spread into Italy, formed the Hittite kingdom of Asia Minor, the Mitannian kingdom in upper Mesopotamia and appeared amongst the Hyksos chiefs in Syria and Egypt. Many attached themselves as tribal aristocracies to indigenous inhabitants.

A second wave, about a thousand years later, brought the Iranians from Transoxiana via the Caucasus. Unlike the majority of the earlier Aryans, who were culturally assimilated, the Iranians retained their identities and, by a slow process of displacement and conquest, gained control of the country that was to bear their name. Associated with them were Cimmerians and Scythians who, remaining as nomads along the routes of migration, provided an important reservoir of mercenaries for the armies of a number of Middle Eastern kingdoms.

The Medes and the Persians were the chief tribes who jostled for the choicest Iranian territories and by the ninth century BC they had established themselves in north-west Iran between Lake Urmia and the plain of Hamadan. Their expansion was arrested for a time by the politically organised world that existed within and beyond the Zagros. In the north-east, around Lakes Van and Urmia, was Urartu, a relatively young but vigorous state, whose Caucasian peoples were related to the Hurrians. On the western edge of the Zagros was the empire of Assyria and, to its south, Babylonia whose capital was the commercial centre of the world. At the head of the Persian Gulf, Elam continued as a fading relic of a once brilliant civilisation already 2,000 years old.

The first historical references to the Medes and Persians

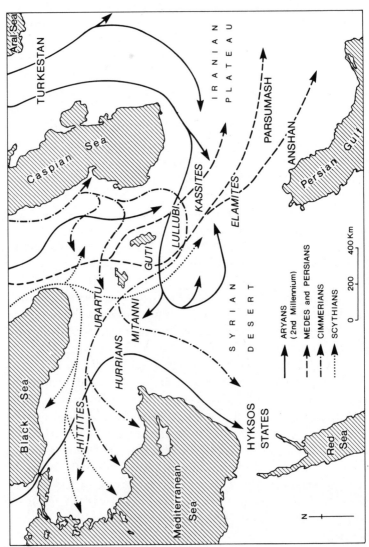

Fig 2 Early folk migrations within the Middle East

appear in Assyrian annals of the ninth century BC. These refer
to the campaign and victories of Shalmaneser who, calling
them all Medes, deported many thousands in 837 BC. Tiglath-
Pileser III and Sargon III also made the Persian and Median
tribes tributary to Assyria. Compared to the nomadic confed-
erations of the hills, Assyria was a rich, powerful and complex
civilisation. Its army was a masterpiece of organisation, comprised of cavalry, light infantry (bowmen and slingers), heavy
infantry (lancers) and a corps of engineers who dug trenches
under enemy walls, built earthen bridges across moats and
smashed gates with heavy battering rams. Such military forces
continually plundered the Zagros tribes, and the Medes and
Persians, though warriors, were no match for their Assyrian
assailants.

### THE KINGDOM OF MEDIA

From their initial homeland in north-west Iran the Persians
moved southwards, but the Medes consolidated their position
and evolved, slowly, from a tribal regime to a village system,
grouping themselves into federations. Repeated raids from
Urartians and Mannians, as well as Assyrians, forced them to
unite in the seventh century BC under a leader who was first
elected but whose title soon became hereditary. The Median
dynasty set up its fortified capital at Ecbatana (Hamadan)
which, according to Herodotus, was founded by Deioces
(Dayakku). In 715 BC he had been carried off to Assyria by
Sargon II, but appears to have recovered his freedom around
708 BC. His kingdom paid tribute to Assyria, though subsequently Deioces was exiled by the Assyrians to Hameth in
Syria.

Phraortes, or Khshathrita (675–653 BC), the successor of
Deioces, united the Median chieftains into a strong confederation and extended authority over the Persian tribes to the
south-west. According to Herodotus, Phraortes attempted,
unsuccessfully, to throw off the Assyrian yoke and an attack on

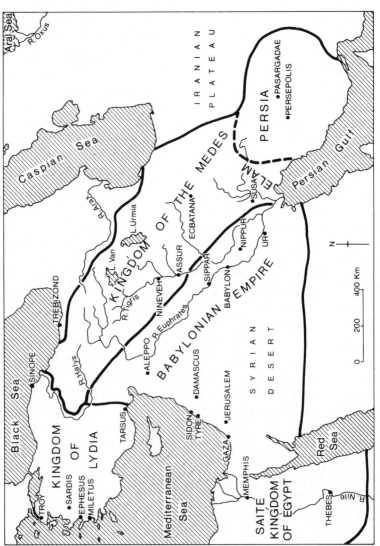

Fig 3  The kingdom of the Medes and neighbouring states

Nineveh cost him his life. It would seem, however, that he was defeated by Scythians and their allies long before he reached Nineveh. These Scythians then dominated Media for twenty-eight years until they were defeated by Phraortes' successor, Cyaxares or Uvakhshtra (653–585 BC). Cyaxares had studied and mastered the techniques and strategies of his enemies and was probably the first ruler to arrange troops according to their weapons—bowmen, spearmen, cavalry, etc. The latter were turned into a lethal striking force and the new model army replaced the old piecemeal tribal expansion by systematic conquest.

## THE FALL OF NINEVEH

Cyaxares' main objective was the westward expansion of Media and the conquest of the Assyrian capital, Nineveh. In wealth and in prestige Nineveh was a tempting prize. The city covered over 1,850 acres (750ha) and was surrounded by 8 miles (12·8km) of thick mud-brick walls faced with stone. Within these walls there were eighteen gates. Assyria had grown weak and the fall of the empire was both desired and predicted. Under Nabopolassar the new Babylonian empire had asserted its freedom from Assyria, but Babylonia's attack on Nineveh in 616 BC proved abortive. Between 614 and 610 the Medes, in alliance with the Babylonians and aided by Scythian mercenaries, sacked Nineveh in a siege that lasted months. Greek traditions and the biblical book of Nahum—an oracle about Nineveh—assert that the capture of this powerfully fortified city was made possible by the flooding of the Tigris, which swept away a section of the walls. According to a Babylonian scribe, the attackers 'carried off the booty of the city, a quantity beyond reckoning, and they turned the city into ruined mounds'.

Nineveh was indeed obliterated. Buildings were burned, palaces and temples levelled, most of the nobles were killed and the women were raped and carried into slavery. Assyrian craftsmen were pressed into forced labour to improve the economies of Babylonia and Media. In addition, the thousands of clay tablets, the records of a great empire, were broken and scattered. 'Seldom,' it has often been said, 'has a people been erased from the face of the earth.' Assyrian territory and spoils were divided equally between Media and Babylonia, and the allied treaty was cemented by the marriage of Amytis, daughter of Cyaxares' son Astyages, to Nebuchadnezzar II, son of Nabopolassar. To comfort Amytis' homesickness for the Median hills, Nebuchadnezzar built the famous 'Hanging Gardens'. This wonder of ancient Babylon was presumably visible from afar and was the crowning grace of the city.

Though Nineveh was destroyed, part of the Assyrian army escaped north-westwards to Harran where Ashur-uballit, a junior member of the royal household, was proclaimed king. Cyaxares was forced to return to Assyria when Ashur-uballit called upon his Egyptian allies for aid. The rebellion was quashed, but Cyaxares' main interest was the conquest of Armenia and Cappodocia in Asia Minor, beyond which lay the rich kingdom of Lydia, a flourishing centre of trade. Though there was some initial conflict with Nabonidus, an officer and later a successor of Nebuchadnezzar, the boundary between the Lydian and Median spheres of influence was fixed at the Halys river (Figure 4).

Excavations in 1965 revealed that Godin was a major Median stronghold, yet the kingdom was ruled from Ecbatana—the 'place of Assembly'. Its situation, at 6,000ft (1,828m) above sea level, and its fortifications both provided protection against expected Assyrian attacks. Herodotus' descriptions of Ecbatana are suspect, but Polybius, though writing later, gives details of its morphology and character. The royal quarters, covering an area of 7 stadia (about ¾ mile (1.2km) in circumference) were situated below the citadel, and its palaces had columns and roofs of cedar and cypress. The woodwork was covered with metal and the roofs had tiles of silver and gold. Throughout subsequent history, Ecbatana remained an important administrative centre within the Persian empire and

a major focus of communications—a function continued by
Hamadan, its modern counterpart.

Though Cyaxares merged Media, parts of Mesopotamia and
eastern Anatolia into a single union, this proved to be merely
the prologue to the empire of the Persians. Migrations and
nomadic wanderings had taken the Persians from the area west
and south-west of Lake Urmia to upland Luristan—the region
east of Elam—and finally to Parsa (Persis or Fars), where they
settled and consolidated. Still under Median domination, their
dynastic line was founded around 700 BC by Hakhamanish or
Achaemenes, whose name was preserved in the royal title of
subsequent Persian kings. The exact chronology is uncertain
(Figure 4), but it appears that his descendant, Teipses, extended
the Persian holdings to include Anshan, originally one of the
princedoms of Elam. The lands of Teipses were divided between his two sons, Ariaramnes (c 640–590 BC) receiving Parsa,
and Kurash or Cyrus I (c 640–600) the western part, including
Anshan which extended to the Mesopotamian lowlands. Ariaramnes is credited with the Achaemenian family's first inscription where, in a cuneiform representation of the Old Persian
language, he declares himself King of Persia, 'a land of fine
horses and good men'.

Persia's territorial expansion lay with the descendants of
Cyrus I. Unlike the Medes, the Persians, in avoiding Assyrian
involvement, had conserved their energy for subsequent strug-
gles. Thus Kanbujiya or Cambyses I (c 600–559 BC) was able to
acquire much of the Elamite territory and proclaim himself
'King of Anshan'. The Persians were still subordinate to the
Median king, Astyages (589–549), though subserviency was
not to last much longer. The marriage of Cambyses to Man-
dane, daughter of Astyages, and the consequent union of the
two royal lines, had unprecedented sequels. Six years after
inheriting his principality of Anshan, Cyrus II, the son of this

marriage, united both parts of the Persian domain by conquering Arsames, son of Ariaramnes. Cyrus then threw off the Median yoke by defeating Astyages (549 BC) and proceeded to Ecbatana. Thus the Achaemenian dynasty established its rule over the kingdom of the Medes and initiated the development of an elaborately organised Persian empire which was to set standards that were imitated by Macedonia and Rome.

# 3

# *The Growth of an Empire*

THE success, the speed and the facility with which the Persian empire was created are largely explained by the youthful energies of the new conquerers and the revolutionary policy of *laissez-faire* that meant tolerance, moderation and permissiveness on a scale hitherto unknown in the ancient world. Assyria and Babylonia, in their relations with subject peoples, had resorted to savage repressions, destroying religious and social institutions and enslaving, sometimes deporting, whole communities. The Persians, on the other hand, respected the traditions and customs of their subjects and authoritarian rule was reduced to a minimum. Provided the law was kept and taxes paid, no attempt was made to press the empire's widely differing peoples, religions and cultures into a common mould. With such a political formula, the Persians believed the old and new could be reconciled, resistance and conflicts diminished, and tendencies towards union fostered and strengthened. Ultimately, however, the magnitude of this ideal hastened the empire's decline, for the talents and contributions of other cultures were preserved and sometimes favoured at the expense of the stability of the state. This, together with centrifugal forces constantly pulling at its heart, brought about its overthrow—but not before the Persians had succeeded in building the largest and most elaborately organised empire the ancient world had seen.

The stages in ancient Persia's history—the drama of its rise and decline—took a course familiar in the history of the Middle

East, where conquest, organisation, stationary maintenance of power, decadence and decline followed in logicaı sequence. Each stage was intimately linked to, and in large measure fashioned by, the personalities of its rulers.

CYRUS THE GREAT

The accession of Cyrus marked the beginnings of Persia's rise to fame and he is regarded as one of the outstanding figures of the Achaemenian dynasty. His success in creating and maintaining the empire was the result of an intelligent blending of diplomatic and military skills, and his rule was tempered with wisdom and tact. The Persians called him 'father'; the Greeks, whom he conquered, saw him as 'a worthy ruler and law-giver', and the Jews regarded him as 'the Lord's anointed'. History has further labelled him as a genius, diplomat, manager, leader of men, the first great propagandist and able strategist.

The conquests of Cyrus followed each other with such rapidity that they have scarcely been equalled, except by Alexander the Great and by the Arabs in the first generation after the death of Mohammed. However, the dominions of Alexander were divided immediately on his death and the Islamic conquests were subjected to great dynastic changes. Such was the initial stability of Cyrus' political system that his territories were not only consolidated on his death but also enlarged by his successors. The reign of Cyrus, therefore, represents the main phase of Persian territorial conquest, and a people—hitherto

The juxtaposition of level upland basins and high mountain ranges is characteristic of the physical geography of the Iranian plateau. This qanat system near Isfahan illustrates the necessity of an adequate water supply to settlement and agriculture

A general view of Persepolis looking west from the hillside of Kuh-i-Rahmat. In the foreground is the Hall of the Hundred Columns with the *apadana* beyond. The entire site covers an area of 33 acres

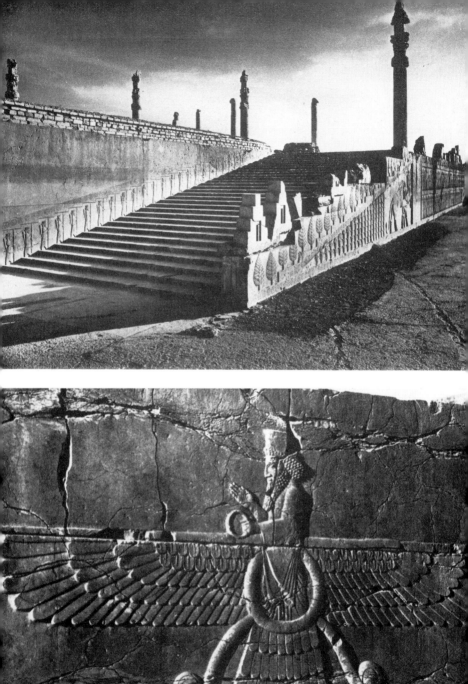

all but unknown—became within thirty years the centre of world history.

Cyrus' expansionist policies were dictated by two objectives: to capture the rich commerce of the eastern littoral of the Mediterranean—the natural terminus of the Asiatic caravans—and to secure the eastern frontier of the empire. Whereas security was the main concern of Cyrus in the east, the immense wealth of the Greek maritime cities of the Ionian coast complemented their value as strategic bases; in addition, they constituted an important reserve of manpower in the form of skilled technicians and expert soldiers. The state of Lydia and the Greek cities were to form an influential element in the commercial and cultural life of the Persian empire.

### LYDIA AND THE GREEKS

Since 585 BC the Halys river had divided Asia Minor between the Lydians to the west and the Medes and Persians to the east (Figure 4). Following the deposition of Astyages, Croesus of Lydia had little confidence that Cyrus would respect this boundary and, seeking alliances with Egypt, Babylonia and Sparta, he challenged the Persian empire. Cappadocia was seized by the Lydians, but Cyrus, in an unexpected winter campaign in 547 BC, and persuaded by the ambiguous replies of the Greek oracles of his victory, re-advanced into Cappodocia. The indecisive battle of Pteria forced Croesus to retreat across the Halys and summon aid from Greece. Cyrus followed and near Sardis, the capital, in spite of stubborn opposition from the Lydian cavalrymen, Croesus was defeated before allied help

The east stairway (sixth-fifth century BC) of the *apadana*, Persepolis. It is decorated with bas-reliefs including a procession of diminutive Persian guards. The columns, surmounted by the remains of bull capitals, supported a high wooden ceiling

Detail of the east door of the Tripylon, Persepolis, showing the winged circlet of Ahura Mazda. The god hovers holding out the coronation wreath in his left hand and raising the right in blessing arrived. Thus the kingdom of Lydia, famed for its riches, passed out of history and the empire of the Persians was extended to cover the greater part of Asia Minor.

The subjugation of the Ionian Greek cities, which had paid allegiance to Lydia, was left to Harpagus. This was accomplished in three years, for they were militarily weak, unable to form a united front, and appeals to Sparta had brought no practical help. Herodotus reveals the science brought to the battlefield by the Persians: neither the Lydian lancers nor the Greek hoplites were a match for the mobile archers or the camel corps of the Persian army. Intrigue and revolt within the Greek cities also aided their reduction and, when Harpagus turned his attention southwards against the Carians, Lycians and Caunians, he marched with Ionian and Aeolian Greeks in his army.

The Greek cities sought from Cyrus the same terms they had enjoyed under Croesus, but Herodotus states that only Miletus was favoured. Though Persian nominees were installed as 'tyrants' in the cities, a measure of self-government was nevertheless maintained. The inclusion of the Greek cities within a young and aggressive empire guaranteed their commercial future. The fact that the Persians encountered little initial resistance was probably partly due to the Greek merchants wishing to expand their commerce as part of a large empire. Already much of their trade lay within the empire or in areas about to be conquered—for example, Al Mina in Syria and Naucratis in Egypt. The Greek island of Samos greatly prospered under the 'tyrant' Polycrates, and its ships ranged freely, sometimes piratically, in the eastern Mediterranean. Polycrates supplied the Persians with manned ships, but his bid for local independence brought the Persian army back to the island before the end of the century.

Cyrus had returned to Persia in triumph before the conquest of Ionia was completed and his wise tolerance is revealed in his treatment of Croesus. It is reported that Croesus was first taken to Persia as a prisoner but subsequently lived as a great noble at the royal court. That he was not put to death seems probable, for Cyrus had also spared the life of Astyages. Croesus and other

Ionians were the first of many foreigners, particularly Greeks, to enter the service of the royal household; for the Persians this was of immense practical and cultural benefit. The conquest of Asia Minor had brought them into contact with a civilisation totally different from their own in government, religion and concepts of life. Though Cyrus showed contempt for the commercial habits of the Greeks, he accommodated their religious institutions and consulted their oracles. Whether by chance or out of respect, most of the oracular replies seemed to favour Persia.

Having completed the conquest of Asia Minor the Persian army turned to the eastern frontiers. Cyrus established suzerainty over the Aryan tribes and built fortifications beyond the Oxus river to the Jaxartes. The peoples of 'Outer Iran' were still nomadic and for further protection Cyrus subdued Parthia, marched against the Bactrian tribes and penetrated as far as Samarkand.

THE FALL OF BABYLON

Neither Babylonia nor Egypt had assisted Lydia against the Persian conquest of Asia Minor, but their tripartite alliance must have prompted Cyrus to deal with the remaining members of it. He had earlier embarked upon preliminary operations against Babylonia, but it was not until 540 BC that the real conquest began. Nabonidus, who through conspiracy had taken the Babylonian throne, failed to maintain internal union, and national security and military affairs had been handed to his son, Belshazzar. Further discontent in Babylonia was provoked by Nabonidus' religious policies, and Cyrus was able to avail himself of this internal division.

The fall of Babylonia can be traced in considerable detail, though it is often difficult to disentangle fact from fiction in various accounts given. Cyrus, it appears, thrust forward over the mountains of Kurdistan and Luristan, capturing Opis and taking Sippar, which surrendered. Once in control of the whole region east of the Tigris he was able to mount an attack on Babylon itself. As a result of the works of Nebuchadnezzar and his successors, the fortifications of the city were impregnable and its resources were such that it had no reason to fear a prolonged siege. Herodotus had visited Babylon and he gives a detailed description of the city and its defences. Built of brick, the walls were some 300ft (91m) high with a circuit of 56 miles (89km). They were surrounded by a moat and pierced by a hundred bronze gates. On the top, along each edge of the wall, a row of buildings was erected with sufficient space between for a four-horse chariot to drive and turn. Within this great wall was a second one, 'not so thick . . . but hardly less strong'.

To capture such a city obviously presented a great problem, but Cyrus' ingenuity was assisted by the revolt of Urbaru (Gobryas), the governor of Gatium, a district to the north of Opis. The fact that Prince Belshazzar was fonder of amusement than of safeguarding his people also aided Cyrus' entry which, according to both Herodotus and Xenophon, was effected by means of a daring piece of strategy. While 'Belshazzar the King made a great feast to a thousand of his lords', the Euphrates, which flowed through Babylon, was diverted by the Persians into a great trench constructed outside the walls. Thus the Persian army, on a night when the Babylonians were engaged in a religious festival, was able to advance into the city along the dry, or at least fordable, river bed. 'Owing to the size of the place,' states Xenophon, 'the inhabitants of the central parts, long after the outer portions of the town were taken, knew nothing of what had changed, but . . . continued dancing and revelling until they learnt the capture but too certainly.' Though there is no justification for rejecting this story, the real reason for the weakness in Babylon's defence was probably due to the revolt of Urbaru.

Babylon reportedly surrendered to Cyrus with scarcely a struggle, and from a contemporary description 'the peoples . . . bowed under him, kissed his feet' and 'were delighted with his sovereignty'. The Babylonian welcome was doubtless not quite so cordial; if there was no resistance it was because the city was taken completely by surprise. Cyrus, however, legitimised his succession as king by 'taking the hand of the god Bel' and his persuasive propaganda convinced the Babylonians that Marmuk, their supreme deity, had directed his steps towards the city. Babylon was neither sacked nor looted and the liberal-minded Cyrus gained local allegiance without disturbing either religious institutions or civil administration. His tolerance is again revealed in his dealings with the Jews who, after captivity in Babylon, were allowed to return to Palestine and rebuild the Temple at Jerusalem.

The Persian conquest of Babylonia inaugurated a new epoch; hitherto, Iran and Anatolia had remained outside the main stream of civilisation. The culture of Babylonia had been predominantly Semitic and Sumerian, and no Mesopotamian king had ruled peoples north-west of Cappadocia—few in fact had crossed the Taurus. Now the ruling power was Iranian—Indo-European—which was to make a major contribution in both government and religion. As king of Babylon, Cyrus also claimed the lands of Phoenicia and Syria, down to the borders of Egypt. Just as Cyrus' first conquest of Media threatened Babylonia, so his last threatened Egypt, but this was left to his son, Cambyses, who reigned as subordinate king of Babylonia.

Though Cyrus retained Susa as his capital and summered at Ecbatana, Babylon from its geographical position continued to function as an administrative centre, central market and intellectual focal point. Cyrus bequeathed to posterity the royal residence of Pasargadae in Parsa, built, according to tradition, on the site of his decisive victory over Astyages. The royal buildings and temples seem to have formed a group of scattered individual pavilions set amidst parks and gardens and surrounded by a wall 13ft (4m) thick. The meaning of Pasargadae—'camp of the Persians'—is probably a faithful picture of what the settlement was like.

Cyrus was continually preoccupied with his eastern frontiers. Nine years after the conquest of Babylon he was killed in battle, though the circumstances of his death are not clear. His eastern opponents appear to have been the Massagetae, a savage people akin to the Scythians, whose domain stretched from the Arax river far into the Russian steppes. Cyrus' body was brought back to Pasargadae; his tomb, which still exists, consisted of a single chamber built on a foundation course of six steps. According to Arrian (AD c 96–180), the body was placed in a golden sarcophagus, and the tomb, as Plutarch (AD c 46–120) reports, bore the inscription: 'O, man, whoever thou art and whencesoever thou comest, for I know that thou wilt come, I am Cyrus, and I won for the Persians their empire. Do not, therefore, begrudge me this little earth which covers my body.'

### CAMBYSES II

Though the early reign of Cambyses II (529–522 BC) is clouded with obscurity, to him is attributable the next phase of Achaemenian expansion which, in accordance with his father's intentions, was the conquest of Egypt. This was essential to the Persian aim for world domination and preparations for the campaign were well in hand before Cambyses ascended the throne. Like Babylon before, the apparent prosperity and activity of Egypt under Psamlik concealed the seeds of its decay; in reality the country lay inert and unable to defend itself. The task of conquest was further lightened by treachery within its boundaries. According to Strabo, Cambyses entered Palestine in 525 BC and mustered his troops at Acre. His passage to Egypt, through Sinai, was assisted by Arabian allies who provided water with the help of camels. The Egyptian forces, defeated at Pelusium, fell back on Memphis and, when this was taken, Egyptian resistance, with the exception of Heliopolis, was at an end. In May 525 BC, Cambyses was acknowledged as the Egyptian king, the legitimate pharaoh, acceptable to the gods of the country. In return for Arabian assistance, the coastal area around Gaza on the Egyptian border, and already under Arab control, was exempted from taxes.

The conquest of Egypt formed only a part of Cambyses' ambitions. Cyrene, a useful stepping-stone to the conquest of

Carthage, readily submitted to the new overlord, but attempts to subjugate the oases of the western desert—beyond Cyrenaica —were abortive and little headway was made in the Nile valley south of Aswan. Cambyses' campaign in Nubia suffered numerous misfortunes which earned for him the titles of 'irresponsible' and 'madman'. Though such comments were probably unjustified, it is generally accepted that he discontinued the enlightened policies of Cyrus. Greek sources speak of his ridicule of the Egyptian religion and the destruction of its temples.

In his absence, the throne of Persia had been seized by Gaumata, personating Smerdis (Bardiya), the king's younger brother—whom Cambyses had secretly assassinated earlier. In all probability the pretender was a Magus—a priest—who knew of the murder. Before reaching Persia, Cambyses died. The circumstances of his death are uncertain. It may have been suicide, or the result of a wound sustained when jumping from his horse. In a bid to gain popularity, Gaumata discontinued military service and the payment of tribute for three years.

DARIUS THE GREAT

With the death of Cambyses and with a pretender on the throne the whole fabric of the empire was endangered. The Medes attempted to restore their initial supremacy over Persia, and the Babylonians aimed at recovering their independence and earlier leadership in the Middle East. The situation was saved by Daryavaush or Darius, son of Hystaspes or Vishtaspa. Though not a direct descendant of Cyrus the Great, he was a distant cousin and a collateral member of the royal house claiming descent from Achaemenes (Figure 4). Darius had joined Cambyses in his Egyptian campaign and had worked his way up to become commander of the Immortals, the royal bodyguard. Well trained in warfare, he modelled himself on Cyrus, though lacking his military genius.

Darius led Cambyses' army back to Persia, and acted swiftly

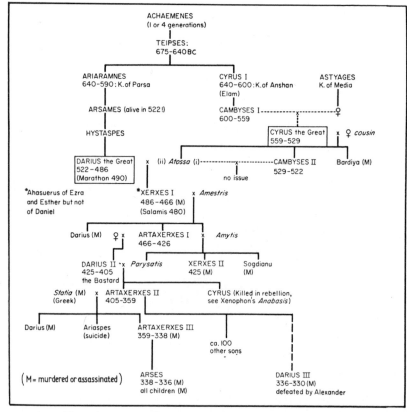

Fig 4  The Achaemenian Dynasty (after Sykes, Olmstead, Girshman, etc)

by defeating and killing Gaumata, but only slowly was he acknowledged as the new king. The first three years of his reign were taken up with subjugating revolts throughout the empire. The most formidable was the rebellion in Babylonia, where Nadintu-Bel proclaimed himself king as Nebuchadnezzar III. Elam, Armenia and Media also revolted, and even Persia, under a second pretender named Vahyazdata, challenged his supremacy. Darius quelled nineteen revolts and defeated nine pretender kings before order was restored.

These events are commemorated by a relief sculptured high on the rock face of Mount Behistun, on the old caravan route between Ecbatana and Babylon. This rock, which towers 3,800ft (1,157m) above the small village of Behistun, is the last peak of a narrow mountain range skirting the plain of Kermanshah on the east. The large relief panel represents Darius crushing beneath his feet the false pretender to the throne, while the nine rebel leaders are led before him in chains. With an upraised hand the king offers his victims to Ahura Mazda, the supreme god of the Persians, symbolised by the winged sun disc and human profile. As part of the relief there are inscriptions in Babylonian (Akkadian), Elamite and Old Persian which read: 'I am Darius the Great King, King of Kings, King of Persia, King of countries, son of Hystaspes, grandson of Arsames, an Achaemenian.' Beneath the panel are many columns of inscriptions relating how Darius gained the crown and put down the rebellious with 'the help of Ahura Mazda and other gods'. Darius' claim that the nineteen battles were accomplished within a year is an exaggeration, but the majority nevertheless took place between the autumn of 522 BC and the spring of 520.

The revolts had plainly revealed the weaknesses of the empire. Darius showed discernment in the choice of his generals and in the deployment of his initially small forces over the various areas of conflict. His campaigns outside Persia added more territories to the empire, taking its boundaries to the Indus and across the Bosporus to Macedonia and Thrace. This latter expedition in 512 BC was directed against the Thracians, Getae and Scythians. Darius then crossed the Danube and led his army through the regions which are now Moldavia and Bessarabia. The motives of this fruitless campaign are obscure, though possibly Darius was interested in obtaining further information about the tribes encountered on the Caspian frontier.

WARS WITH GREECE

The closing years of Darius' reign saw the outbreak of the Graeco–Persian wars which were to be disastrous to the empire but profoundly influenced the course of Greek history.

In 499 BC the Greek cities of Ionia—under Persian rule since 546 BC—rebelled and drove out the tyrannical governors established by the Persians. An army of Milesians, aided by Athenians and Eretrians, took and burnt Sardis. For the Greeks, the Persian wars, which unjustifiably assumed the form of a crusade against democracy, had begun. Darius, after trying to find a peaceful outcome to the conflict, sent a fleet of 600 Egyptian, Phoenician and Cypriot vessels which defeated the Ionian navy. Miletus, the leading city of the Ionian coast, was sacked and its people were deported to the banks of the Tigris. By abandoning the systems of tyrannies set up by Cyrus, and replacing them with democratic governments and a large measure of autonomy, Darius appeased the Ionian cities which promptly renounced their close alliance with Athens.

Persia thus gained victory in the first round, but Darius was not satisfied. In 490 BC he mounted attacks on the Greek mainland in reprisal for their aid to the Ionian revolt. By clever diplomatic action he further divided the Greek states, which already had conflicting economic and political interests. Many looked to him for protection. Only Athens and Sparta resolved to defend themselves against Persian ascendancy. The punitive Persian expedition which plundered Eretria was unable to take Athens. Darius sent a fleet of transports to the coast of Attica and 30,000 troops disembarked in the bay of Marathon, 19 miles (32km) north-west of Athens. The Persians had expected treason from within to open the gates of Athens, but the scheme failed and the Athenians, with a force of 10,000 led by Miltiades, routed the invaders as they re-embarked at Marathon, before Spartan help arrived. A runner brought the news of the victory to Athens.

Militarily, Marathon was of small importance but its effect on the morale of Greece was enormous. 'These men were the first Greeks,' says Herodotus, 'who had the courage to face up to Persian dress and the men who wore it, whereas up to that time the very name of the Persians brought terror to a Greek.' When the Persians again attempted the conquest of Greece, their leader was Xerxes and something like a united Greek army was there to meet him with the ability to crush Darius' dream of a universal empire.

Darius I died in 486 BC. He was buried in a rock-hewn tomb at Naqsh-i-Rustan, a few miles north-east of Persepolis. His tomb bears trilingual inscriptions which relate his personal views of his achievements and character: 'Says Darius the king: By the favour of Ahura Mazda I am of such a sort that I am a friend to right, I am not a friend to wrong; it is not my desire that the weak man should have wrong done to him by the mighty; nor is it my desire that the mighty should have wrong done to him by the weak.'

The reign of Darius represents the second major phase in the empire's history. His genius lay principally in the field of administration and under him the Persian empire attained the height of its power and glory. He ruled a vast area from Egypt and the Aegean Sea to the Indus and Jaxartes rivers, and from the Persian Gulf to the Black and the Caspian Seas. This was an empire which clearly aimed at including the whole civilised world in a single political unit. Under Darius it was organised along lines which were to continue until 330 BC when the last Persian king fell before Alexander the Great.

In the manner of Cyrus, Darius set himself the ideal of ruling as a benevolent despot. The Behistun inscriptions are a kind of credo glorifying the enlightened imperialism of a just and merciful monarch. One of the most famous figures in antiquity, his epithet 'great' was acknowledged by Persians and foreigners alike. Aeschylus, in *The Persians*, displays his admiration for Darius, as do Herodotus and other Greek writers.

### XERXES

Throughout the next century and a half (486–338 BC) the successors of Darius were chiefly concerned with the preservation of the empire which he had consolidated and organised. The reign of Xerxes (the Ahasuerus of the books of Ezra and

Esther) marks the third main stage in Achaemenian civilisation—the stationary maintenance of power prior to real decadence and decline. Xerxes, the former viceroy of Babylonia, was thirty-five years old when he ascended the throne. Many of his administrative measures were sound but, unlike Darius, he had little talent for economics and revelled too much in court pleasures. He was a luxury-loving monarch, who built monuments and palaces.

Xerxes successfully quelled the revolt in Egypt, but toleration as displayed by Cyrus and Darius was discarded in favour of conformity which was brutally enforced. His actions to avenge the murder of the Babylonian satrap (viceroy) were equally drastic. Babylon's walls were razed, its temples destroyed and the gold statue of the god Bel was melted down. The sacking of Babylon was so thorough and extensive that the city never recovered its ancient splendour and much of its trade was diverted to Egypt. Babylon's destruction, the result of Xerxes' undisciplined temper, had fatal consequences for the Persian empire. Another major error of judgement was his abandonment of the universalism professed by Darius and his propagation of Persian nationalism. Xerxes declared himself a Persian king inspired by Ahura Mazda only and not a sovereign based on divine right granted by other gods—for example, Marduk or Ammon. His court was no longer cosmopolitan, but Persian.

### DEFEAT BY THE GREEKS

The Greek city states remained restless and their renewed struggle with Persia was imminent. Xerxes' ambition was the annihilation of Greece. In 480 BC, ten years after Marathon, a massive Persian army marched through Thrace, Macedonia and Thessaly, and a fleet sailed along the Greek coasts. According to Herodotus, the land troops numbered 24,000 and the fleet of 1,200 ships included Phoenician, Ionian, Egyptian and Cypriot squadrons. The movement of such vast forces required great organisation. The construction of a bridge of boats across the Hellespont for the passage of troops was a major feat of engineering, and provision stations were established at various points along the north coast of the Aegean. To avoid sending his fleet around the dangerous promontory of Athos, Xerxes ordered a canal to be dug through the isthmus of Sane. A mile and a half (2.5km) long and wide enough for two warships to be rowed abreast, the canal took labourers, driven with whips, three years to complete. Herodotus regarded the operation as a piece of ostentation on Xerxes' part, for it would have been perfectly feasible, he comments, to have dragged the ships across the isthmus on rollers.

The Persian army was temporarily halted at the Pass of Thermoplyae on the Gulf of Lamia by a small but heroic force of Spartans and Boeotians. The Persians then pressed southwards, taking Thebes, and on to Athens, where they took the evacuated city and burned the Acropolis. The Athenians, however, had occupied the nearby island of Salamis where the allied ships were stationed. The Persian fleet, lured into the narrows, was overwhelmed and retreated across the Aegean. The Greeks again successfully challenged them near Miletus, and a large part of Asiatic Greece was freed from Persian control and admitted to the mainland league. In the following year (479 BC) there was a further decisive victory by the Greeks at Plataea in the north. As far as Greece was concerned, the Persian menace was effectively removed, for Xerxes was forced to relinquish all his possessions beyond Asia Minor. He was assassinated in his palace in 466 BC.

PERIOD OF DECLINE

The three succeeding Achaemenian sovereigns maintained relatively peaceful reigns and managed to preserve the autonomy of the empire for about sixty years. The accession of Artaxerxes II in 405 BC marked its real decline. The incompetence of subsequent rule, the revolts, wars and court intrigues collectively undermined the power of the 'King of Kings' and brought about the downfall of the Persian colossus (see Chapter 9).

# 4

# *Government and Organisation*

CYRUS created the Persian empire, but Darius was largely responsible for its rationalisation on a sound administrative basis. Hitherto empires had been organised in a rudimentary fashion. Darius, by adapting Assyrian, Babylonian and Egyptian precedents, and in devising a great deal more, succeeded in initiating a model form of provincial government. His policies involved the delicate balancing of feudal and autonomist forces on the one hand with decentralising authority on the other, in an attempt to synthesise varied peoples and cultures in a single government. His ideal was to impress upon every one of his subjects not only the rights and privileges of the state but also its burdens and responsibilities. The immense cultural amalgam that constituted the Persian empire needed monarchical power as a basis of unity. Darius ascended the throne as an absolute monarch—a hereditary quasi-feudal king—enjoying religious sanction and claiming power through the will of the gods.

## THE PERSIAN MONARCHY

Kingship and royalty were alien institutions among the Aryan forebears, whose leaders were elected by tribal discretion. Subsequently, it probably became customary for the descendants of popular headmen to succeed their kinsmen, giving rise to a dominant family or clan within each federation. The principle of a ruling class was firmly established when Cyrus acceded, yet through diplomacy—rather than by absolute power—other tribes were won to his leadership. By Darius' time the office of king was the highest authority throughout the empire, and the royal personage was the symbol of imperial unity. This conception of monarchy, characteristic throughout the East, was based on the theory that the gods delegated someone as their representative among men. In times of peace such a dignitary acted as a chief priest, but in wartime he either became a military leader or found some more vigorous representative to fight on his, and the god's, behalf. Military power often increased at the expense of religion and ritual; feuds between political and ecclesiastical authority constantly characterised Middle Eastern kingdoms. In Egypt, for example, the priesthood of Ammon, god of Thebes, grew politically and economically powerful, and successfully challenged the rule of the pharaohs. The power of the priests in relation to the Persian sovereigns is evident from the hostility they showed to Cambyses and, in contrast, the favour they showed to Darius.

Successful kingship depended on diplomacy with the priesthood. Darius, though proclaimed king by divine right, was not, like the Assyrian kings, a despot whose absolutism was derived from his national god. Through his tolerance and acceptance of the religions of his subject peoples, Darius became the representative of their gods. In Persia he claimed descent from Ahura Mazda; in Babylon from Marduk, and in Egypt from Ammon and 'begotten of Ra'. In parts of his empire where no dynastic theory existed he introduced his own with the aid of Persian magi. Thus the great temples of Ephesus and Sardis, economic as well as religious centres, were manned by Persian priests who introduced the monotheistic code of Zoroaster (see Chapter 8).

Such toleration went much further than mere lip-service to foreign gods. The Persian kings were actively involved in the temple worship of alien deities. In Egypt, for example, Darius sacrificed to the local gods and especially honoured Apis. He, like his predecessors, also contributed to the building of temples and conferred privileges on priesthoods and religious institutions. Cyrus and Darius not merely permitted the rebuilding of the Jewish Temple at Jerusalem, but laid the cost of it on the royal treasury.

The Persian kings were obviously confronted with religious difficulties, but the strength of the monarchy and the conviction that the king was god's elect were forces too powerful for such dualism to become significant. Whether the monarchy was faithful to Zoroastrianism is debatable, for foreign gods were brought within the system of the Persian supreme religion. The priests disapproved of these syncretisms and their disapproval probably led to the usurption of the throne by the Magus Gaumata under whose orders many temples of local deities were destroyed.

### CENTRAL GOVERNMENT

The main threat to the throne was not the priesthood but vassal rulers rising to power in the provinces. Thus a Persian ruler's title to kingship was first and foremost his ability as an army leader and conqueror. With the continual expansion of the empire, his main objective was to effectively control distant parts of his domain. Based on unquestioned central authority, this was achieved by a powerful bureaucracy radiating to every corner of the empire.

The nobles who had conspired to give Darius the throne, following Gaumata's rebellion, were rewarded by being elevated to special status—that is, an aristocratic hierarchy of bureaucrats on whom the king depended for support. Their families, along with the royal line, became the chief houses of Persia and the inner circle of the royal court. From them Darius selected

Some of the most famous bas-reliefs at Persepolis are those depicting the procession of peoples from the empire's twenty-three lands, bringing gifts and tributes to the king. This detail shows the Bactrian delegation

Persepolis: East stairway of the Apadana. Bas-reliefs from sixth-fifth centuries BC depicting other representatives of the empire's lands in the tribute procession before the King of Kings.

his wives. Although oaths and ties of blood bound the families to the throne, at the same time their power presented a challenge that could not be ignored. For example, Otanes, according to Herodotus, was as absolute within his own dominions as the king himself. Darius, however, although the tool of feudal reaction, proved to be a politician and diplomat of genius. Though 'the king of the Persians might do whatsoever he desired', he had great regard both for law and custom, and little was done without consultation with the Persian nobles and court officials.

The nerve centre of the empire was the imperial court. The King's body of councillors were, in all probability, chosen in Darius' time from the 'seven families'—the Book of Esther names the seven chiefs of the Medes and Persians who could view the face of the king. Ezra, in the letter given to him by Artaxerxes, is described as sent to Judaea by 'the king and his seven councillors', and these seven are again associated with the king in the gift to the Temple at Jerusalem.

The institution of prime minister, as a supreme representative of the king, does not seem to have existed among the early Achaemenian kings. There is some evidence, however, that administrative control was in the hands of an officer known in Old Persian as the *Hazarapatis* and in Greek as the *Chiliarch*. There seems little development beyond this point and the king jealously guarded his position as universal ruler. In addition to his council, the king—Darius in particular—surrounded himself with people drawn from all parts of the empire—Greeks, Jews, Babylonians and Egyptians; these were collaborators (architects, doctors, generals, engineers, admirals) rather than councillors. Babylonian scribes were certainly responsible for financial administration, and the subsequent Seleucid office of *epistolographos* probably referred to the head scribe of the chancellery.

Scenes of lions attacking bulls are common in Achaemenian art and may represent some cosmic event (related to the spring equinox) or allude to royal power. This reproduced panel of the original at Persepolis reveals the finely chiselled details of both animals

## THE ROYAL CAPITALS

Five royal capitals were needed to accommodate the court on its progress from one part of the empire to another. According to Toynbee and other scholars, the peripatetic nature of the Achaemenian royal court was related to the problems of governing and controlling the vast domain. Climatic factors, too, may have necessitated the establishment of winter, spring and summer quarters.

Susa and Babylon, both ancient cities that pre-dated the empire, were the main administrative capitals; Ecbatana, the old Median capital, 6,000ft (1,828m) above sea level, was a summer retreat; Pasargadae, founded by Cyrus, acted for a time as the seat of coronation; and Persepolis, under Darius and later kings, became the dynastic capital and the setting for the important New Year celebrations. The traditional homeland of the Persians, however, failed to offer a good site for the capital of a great empire and neither Pasargadae nor Persepolis proved suitable administrative centres. It is doubtful whether they could be termed cities in the true sense—Herzfeld described Pasargadae as a settlement of nomads around a royal residence.

Cyrus belonged to the *Pasargadae* clan and built his summer capital in its homeland. He perhaps wintered in Borazjan, at least until the capture of Babylon. Previously the Elamites, to escape the intense heat of the Mesopotamian plains, established their summer capital at Tepe Maliyan, in Anshan, and wintered at Susa. Darius, in the same tradition, chose Persepolis as a summer residence and Susa as his winter capital. Both became the symbols of the might and glory of the empire, and no expense was spared on the construction and adornment of their palaces.

Persepolis is shrouded with considerable mystery for it remained unknown to the Greeks before Alexander and its name is not mentioned in Babylonian, Phoenician, Egyptian or

Jewish records. In the later Middle Ages there was much confusion over the site of Persepolis. It was generally equated with the modern town of Shiraz, while the actual ruins of the Achaemenian palace (locally known as Chehel Minar, 'The Forty Pillars') were identified as the courts of Jamshid. Not until 1618 was the correct identity of Persepolis made by the Spanish ambassador to Persia, Garcia Silva Figueroa, who recognised it from descriptions by ancient authors such as Diodorus and Plutarch.

In spite of its enigmatic character, Persepolis was where New Year and other celebrations were held by Darius and Xerxes, though the later kings used it less as a capital and more as a private retreat. By the time of Xenophon the court spent seven winter months in Babylon, two summer months in Ecbatana and three spring months in Susa. The only indication that Persepolis retained some political importance is that it was burned by Alexander the Great after his forces had fought their way to the palace through a barrage of brigand tribesmen. The destruction of Persepolis on Alexander's part, however, may merely have been a symbolic act of aggression to mark the end of the Achaemenian dynasty.

The continuation of Ecbatana as a royal capital was partly due to its favourable summer climate and partly to its historic prestige as the former Median capital. Within the Achaemenian empire the Medes remained second only to the Persians in the hierarchy of imperial peoples. Moreover, Ecbatana occupied a strategically important position on the great northern trade route where it dropped to the level of the Iranian plateau after crossing the Zagros ranges. This whole north-eastern region was one of high priority in the Achaemenian affairs of state.

Because of its geographical location and economic power, Babylon was used by the Achaemenians as a political capital, but it was Susa that became the empire's real administrative centre. The transference of central government from Parsa to Susa was a step taken by Darius around 521 BC and the fame of his building programmes, recorded in classical writings, has now been corroborated by archaeological excavations. In addition to its strategic situation in relation to the Zagros uplands and the Mesopotamian plains, Susa was also the most centrally placed of the Achaemenian royal capitals, being 217 miles (350km) south of Ecbatana, 233 miles (375km) south-east of Babylon and about 311 miles (500km) north-west of Persepolis and Pasargadae. Yet Susa remained an awkward seat of government for an empire that extended to the Jaxartes, Indus, Nile and, less permanently, the Danube.

PROVINCIAL GOVERNMENT

While centralised government was common to most Middle East civilisations, provincial administration—of which the Persian empire provides an early example—was more of a departure from the traditions of the past. Within the Achaemenian government, the system produced a duality between absolute monarchy and powerful provincial rulers, a pattern which continued as part of Persian government down to the end of the nineteenth century.

The foundations of the provincial system of government were laid by Cyrus and Cambyses, but the deliberate policy of administrative *laissez faire* proved a major factor behind the widespread insurrections that broke out in 522 BC. To insure himself and his successors against rebellion, Darius re-organised the empire into provinces or *satrapies*, each governed by a viceroy or *satrap* ('protector of the kingdom') whom the king appointed from among the royal princes and nobles. Some satrapies were purely artificial creations, but others, though not drawn according to former national boundaries, were conceived as cultural and economic units. Such a system provided the basis for the distribution of royal commands and facilitated the organisation of defence and collection of taxes.

There is conflicting evidence about the number of satrapies created by Darius between those mentioned by Herodotus and the lists which appear chiefly in Darian inscriptions at Behistun, Persepolis, Naqsh-i-Rustan, Susa and elsewhere.

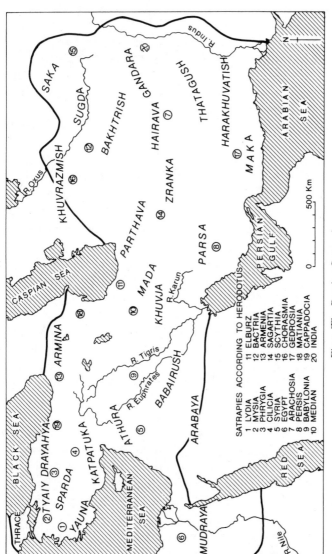

Fig 5 The Persian Satrapies

SATRAPIES ACCORDING TO HERODOTUS

| 1 LYDIA | 11 ELBURZ |
| 2 MYSIA | 12 BACTRIA |
| 3 PHRYGIA | 13 ARMENIA |
| 4 CILICIA | 14 SAGARTIA |
| 5 SYRIA | 15 SCYTHIA |
| 6 EGYPT | 16 CHORASMIA |
| 7 ARACHOSIA | 17 GEDROSIA |
| 8 PERSIS | 18 MATIANIA |
| 9 BABYLONIA | 19 CAPPADOCIA |
| 10 MEDIAN | 20 INDIA |

The Book of Daniel inflates their number to 120, but the traditionally held view, chiefly based on Herodotus, fixes the figure in the low twenties—this was following the conquest of India (the Punjab) and included Thrace, which was lost by Xerxes. Several scholarly works, the most detailed being that of Toynbee, have attempted to correlate the names that appear in monumental inscriptions with the satrapal list given by Herodotus. There is some doubt, however, as to whether the monumental lists refer to provinces; G. G. Cameron maintains that they enumerate groups of people whom Darius and Xerxes thought worthy of specific mention.

The earliest list of peoples making up the empire of Darius is given in the Behistun inscription. These twenty-three regional names are shown in Figure 5—for purposes of comparison, the ringed numerals refer to the satrapal list of Herodotus. In roughly cyclical order, beginning with the central provinces, the regions on the inscribed list are: Parsa (Persis); Khuvja (Elam); Babairush (Babylonia); Athura (Assyria); Arabaya (the north-eastern portion of Arabia); Mudraya (Egypt); Tyaiy Drayahya (the 'sea lands' on the northern coast of Asia Minor); Sparda (Sardis and Lydia); Yauna (the Ionian Greek settlements on the west coast of Asia Minor); Mada (Media); Armina (Armenia); Katpatuka (Cappadocia); Parthava (Parthia); Zranka (Drangiana—the area around Lake Hilmend); Hairava (Areia—the region of modern Herat); Khuvrazmish (Chorasmia); Bakhtrish (Bactria); Sugda (Sogdia—modern Samarkand); Gandara (northern Punjab); Saka (the steppe-lands east of Bactria); Harakhuvatish (Arachosia); Thatagush (south-west of Gandara); Maka (on the Arabian Sea coast). A further seven regions were mentioned by Xerxes or late in Darius' reign. The large provincial areas recorded on Behistun were apparently subdivided into smaller units, particularly in Asia Minor.

The provincial governors, or satraps, were generally men of high birth, normally members of the imperial family either through birth or marriage. They were appointed for indefinite periods, sometimes for life, and in a number of provinces the office became hereditary, though it was terminable at the will of the king. According to Xenophon, the basic philosophy of satrapal government was embodied in the command given by Cyrus to his viceroys: 'to imitate me'. This was often done with pomp and ceremony which equalled that of the royal court, and the satrap governed as a minor king. He had full control of civil administration and his province was a judicial district of which he was the head. The satrap's duties included the maintenance of security, the administration of economic policies, and the collection and despatching of taxes and tribute for the royal treasury. Where the more important satrapies were subdivided, the governors of these districts carried out similar duties. In other regions, traditional or local forms of government were perpetuated—as in the case of the Phoenician states of the Levant, the Greek states of Asia Minor and the Jews under high-priestly supervision.

Darius, aware of potential satrapal rebellion, introduced measures that increased central control. Media, Armenia, and Babylonia, together with western Anatolia, all examples of nationalist-minded viceroyalties, were consequently subdivided respectively into four, three, two and two taxation districts. This reduced the likelihood of a traitorous satrap or an insurgent pretender gaining control of an entire province. Rapid communications (see Chapter 5) provided a further safeguard, and independent action was hardly possible without prior reference to Susa. An imperial secretary, attached to each satrap, reported directly to the central government; he attended to the receipts and despatches of royal correspondence, and was apparently an *ex-officio* member of the provincial council. The councillors were nobles who supported, or challenged, the rulings of the satrap.

Though forces were raised and supervised within the satrapies, the Achaemenians separated civil from military rule. Thus, at every key position in the empire, troops were stationed and commanded by independent generals. As a final security measure, satraps and generals were supervised by high officials, expressively nicknamed the 'Eyes and the Ears of the

King'. These travelled widely, accompanied by their own private forces; their periodic and unexpected visits to satrapies to examine local affairs were much admired by the monarchs of antiquity. This institution, which Darius probably borrowed from Egypt, was subsequently adopted by Charlemagne.

A measure of Darius' genius as an organiser was his ability to keep at least twenty powerful governors—and potential rivals—under control. It is uncertain whether new satrapies were created after his reign, but there were redistributions of authority within the existing administrative framework and frequent boundary changes. The whole development, however, is obscured by the lack of information and confused by the conflicting nomenclature given to high officials in the Greek sources. It is debatable whether the Persians succeeded in imposing more than a semblance of unity on the empire. One factor in its decline was certainly rebellions in semi-autonomous satrapies, but the system remained as the form of provincial government until the conquest of Persia by Alexander. It was then taken over and turned to good account by the Hellenic successor states.

### TRIBUTE AND TAXATION

Persian expenses were heavy. They involved the maintenance and construction of palaces, the upkeep of imperial magnificence, the management of royal domains and the general administration of both civil and military affairs. The king had unfettered control over all provincial revenues in the form of taxes, dues, corvees, booty, tribute and gifts. This wealth was hoarded, some of it occasionally used to make loans or to finance profitable operations. Both central and provincial government was financed by taxes and tribute. A major function of the satrap, and one which greatly contributed to his power, was control of revenue. Darius inherited a haphazard tax structure in which irregular methods of collection varied from one province or region to another. Based on a carefully organised survey of the wealth of each province, Darius regulated the amount of taxes, in produce or money, that were payable to each satrap and to the royal treasury. Persia itself, as the homeland of the royal house, was tactfully omitted from the tax system, but voluntary contributions were expected and, on a fiscal plane, the distinction between 'Persians' and other peoples was little more than a formality. Furthermore the Persians were required to provide troops and military leaders, for they were the backbone of the Achaemenian army.

In Darius' time, taxes on agricultural produce might have amounted to roughly 20 per cent of the value of the crops on a given estate. Other primary and secondary industries—such as fishing, mining, textiles—were similarly assessed. A generous sum was given to each satrap for the maintenance of his vice-regal court and the remainder went to the imperial treasuries at Susa, Ecbatana and Persepolis. The most common forms of payment were precious metals apportioned in basic units of weight, of which the largest unit, the *talent*, was the traditional measure of the ancient world. In Persia it weighed 66lb (30kg). Its value was enormous. In terms of modern currency a silver talent was worth about £1,050; a half talent would pay the entire 200-man crew of an oared warship for a month. The gold talent was worth approximately thirteen times that of the silver and because of its high value it was used in major transactions only. The talent was subdivided into 60 *minas*, and the *mina* into 60 *shekels* and 100 *drachmas*, each drachma weighing one-seventh of an ounce.

Satrapal taxes were paid in talents. The lowest amounts came from some of the extensive but thinly populated provinces: Arachosia, for example, contributed 170 Babylonian talents of silver, and Elburz and Matiania 200 silver talents each. The highest taxes were 360 talents of gold dust from India; 1,000 silver talents from Assyria and from Babylonia; 700 from Egypt and other African dominions, and 450 from Media. The four Asia Minor satrapies collectively paid 1,760 silver talents. Darius collected almost 15,000 silver talents a year, according to Herodotus; after defraying annual costs and outgoings, this accumulation of wealth by the royal treasuries persisted for a further two centuries. Alexander the Great found 380,000 talents of silver in the treasury at Ecbatana—and this was after the royal reserves had been extensively drained by Darius III to finance the war with Macedonia. It is further reported that Darius III, in his flight, carried with him 8,000 talents. The amount of tax and tribute was out of all proportion to what was spent on the satrapies themselves. The normal levy was regularly raised and ultimately the taxation system, together with the hoarding of wealth, contributed to the decline and fall of the empire.

Goods and services were also rendered to the royal courts. Passages in the books of Ezra and Nehemiah make a distinction between fixed annual taxes, contributions in kind and way-tolls. Contributions in kind were necessary to support the army, the royal household, the satraps and even sub-satraps. Herodotus records that Babylonia supported the king and his army for four months in the year and the rest of 'Asia' for the remaining eight months. The extent and value of contributions in kind cannot be estimated. The Arabs gave 6,600lb (3,000kg) of frankincense annually, the Egyptians provided 1,500 horses, 50,000 sheep and 2,000 mules, and these figures were almost doubled by Media. Babylonia was forced to pay a grim annual tribute of 500 castrated boys, who were sent to serve as eunuchs in the Persian aristocratic houses. A similar fate followed the conquest of the Aegean islands of Chios and Lesbos when youths were castrated and girls sent to Persian harems. The Persepolis reliefs graphically illustrate the various types of tribute brought to the king, which probably amounted to two or three times the sum of fixed monetary taxes. In addition to these regular levies there were harbour and market tariffs, road tolls and duties on almost anything that could be made a profitable enterprise.

### THE LAW OF THE MEDES AND PERSIANS

The king, the source of political power, was also the lawgiver. Persian law was immutable and irrevocable except when applied to the royal personage. Yet tradition bound the king to consult with high officials before arriving at crucial decisions, especially when these meant bending the law for 'royal' purposes. Herodotus relates how Cambyses, wishing to marry his sister, consulted his council as to whether such a match was permissible. Careful not to anger the king, the council replied that, though no law could be found condoning incest, one did exist which allowed a Persian king to do whatever he pleased. Cambyses was satisfied.

Before the reign of Darius, Achaemenian law was a complicated mixture of many local systems, yet the fame of Persian justice is recorded in the Greek sources. A number of clay tablets from various archaeological sites provide a glimpse of Cyrus' judicial system. They record the deeds and sentence of Grimilli, a serf employed by one of the temples. Grimilli, it appears, was a compulsive animal thief and grafter who was finally brought to justice in September 538 BC. The court, composed of high officials at Uruk, ruled that restitution be made to the tune of sixty animals for every one stolen, together with a monetary fine. Such a sentence was nonetheless light for, in general, Persian punishment was severe and often ended in death, mutilation or banishment. The greatest crime was rebellion or revolt against the throne, but judicial corruption was considered equally serious. Under Cambyses a judge was executed for taking a bribe and his skin was used to cover the judgement seat. Apparently this judicial office was hereditary and the act was a warning to his son. Another report mentions that Darius sentenced a dishonest judge to be crucified. He was taken from the cross only after careful consideration of another of the king's laws—that one wrong deed in a man's life might be pardoned if it was outweighed by a record of good.

Emphasis on truth and justice formed the basis of the Darian legal system.

No actual Persian law code has been found, but some scholars have attempted to assemble its framework from a variety of non-legal sources, including the Old Testament which refers to the 'law of the Medes and Persians which altereth not'. It is now believed that the Persians, rather than advancing their own philosophy, extended and developed the use of existing Middle Eastern legal concepts—particularly the Babylonian code of Hammurabi, who lived around 1700 BC. He was not only a great military commander but also an outstanding administrator and lawgiver. The provisions of his code touched on every aspect of life—commercial, social, domestic and moral—and its personal decrees advocated an 'eye for an eye' philosophy. As a universal code it survived the ruin of the Babylonian empire and remained the foundation, especially, of commercial law until the time of the Roman empire.

Darius' personal credo is made clear from a number of royal inscriptions: 'What is right I love and what is not right I hate. The man who decides for a Lie I hate . . . And whoever injures, according to what he has injured, I punish . . . Of the man who speaks against the truth, never do I trust a word.'. Like Hammurabi before him, Darius deemed it particularly important that 'the stronger does not smite nor destroy the weak', though hearsay was not enough to convict an accused person. Social tribunals dealt with items such as family inheritance and property issues, and customary law was used in these judgements. The state or royal tribunals, however, interpreted the king's law on issues such as taxation and crimes against the government, its officers and its property. Royal judges served for life and the king, the chief judge, also functioned as a court of appeal. Though subject peoples retained their own legal systems side by side with that of Darius, his laws remained in force long after the collapse of the empire.

### THE ARMY

Under Cyrus the army was largely composed of Persian militia who had supported his rebellion against the Medes. After the conquest, a complex military establishment was created, made up of a number of nationalities with differing methods of warfare and a variety of weapons. An army of this dimension was only needed in the event of a serious war effort, but musters and manoeuvres were held periodically within the satrapies, which were also regimental bases. Despite the construction and improvement of roads, which speeded up marches and aided the movement of supplies, the mobilisation of regional forces took an excessively long time.

The flower of this army were the Persians and Medes, who manned the garrisons at key points throughout the empire—at river crossings, mountain passes and on routes connecting provincial capitals with frontiers. This standing force—relatively small in numbers in view of its wide commitments—was used, in Darius' time, to suppress internal revolts. The militia before the throne of Darius—sculpted on the staircase at Persepolis—are shown alternately as Persians and Medes. In the army of Xerxes, Iranians again head the list of national contingents. All army units, whether Iranian or not, were commanded by either Persians or Medes: the Assyrians by Otaspes, the Indians by Pharnazathres, and the Arabians and Ethiopians by Arsames, a son of Darius. City garrisons, too, were manned and commanded principally by Persians. At Sardis, for example, Oroites had a bodyguard of 1,000 Persian spearmen, and the garrison at Memphis, which was larger, consisted chiefly of Persians and assorted mercenaries. An important frontier garrison existed at Doriscus, on the Thracian coastal road from the Hellespont to mainland Greece. After Xerxes' disastrous attempt in 480–479 BC to unite the Hellenic world under Achaemenian rule, this garrison became the sole surviving fragment of an earlier province west of the Hellespont and east of the river Strymon. Although the north-eastern frontier, where Cyrus met his death, must always have been the most critical and important, there is no evidence of garrisons for its defence. However, through a military alliance, parts of this frontier were screened by a nomadic horde which had developed a type of feudal nobility throughout the broad territories and which strongly resisted the forces of Alexander the Great.

The standing army was maintained and controlled by the central government. The kings were generous in rewarding distinguished service. Following the Assyrian precedent, officers and soldiers were awarded special titles or ranks for bravery and service. Robes of honour, special daggers or bracelets of honour, but more especially grants of land, became general marks of merit. As a result of land grants in provincial territories, the Iranian feudal nobility proliferated, thus aiding governmental control. This policy of 'planting' feudal baronies of the ruling nation was later applied with thoroughness by, among others, the Ottoman empire.

The king's bodyguard, known as the Immortals, were the cream of this standing army. Probably originating from those Persian detachments supporting Darius when he attained the throne, they were chosen from among Elamites as well as Persians and Medes. The Immortals were so called because every fallen member of this élite corps was immediately replaced by a new recruit, so that the strength of 10,000 men remained constant. Their appearance is illustrated in the Persepolis reliefs and the glazed brick friezes at Susa—though this ceremonial attire bore little resemblance to what they would have worn in battle. Each carried a spear of cornel wood (a hard timber of the dogwood family) tipped with a silver blade and bearing a distinctive golden pomegranate on the handle. From the shoulder hung a bow and a quiver of arrows. The sartorial elegance of the Immortals was beyond compare. Their flowing robes were light purple and yellow with brown stars or squares; their leather shoes, laced or buttoned, were blue or yellow; green braid tied back their hair; beards were short and tightly curled; bracelets and earrings completed their adornment.

At its peak the full army comprised 360,000 men, perfectly organised into six corps (each of 60,000), made up of six divisions (10,000) sub-divided into battalions (1,000), companies (100) and squads (10). The troops were grouped according to their weapons as lancers, archers and cavalry; each ethnic contingent retained its traditional armour, headdress and weapons. There were helmets of bronze, wood, leather, foxskin and woven wicker; leather jackets, cloaks and flowing robes. The Ethiopians smeared their bodies with chalk and vermilion, and draped themselves in lion and leopard skins. Weapons included spears, javelins, battleclubs, daggers, palm-ribbed spears, stone-tipped arrows, lassoes, and spears tipped with sharpened antelope-horn. On the battlefield, the Iranians rode horses; the Libyans and Egyptians attacked in chariots; the Arabs fought on camels. Although, as Herodotus affirms, this may not have increased its efficiency, the array of these varied ethnic troops—and perhaps other unco-ordinated levies—undoubtedly attested to the role of Persia as a universal state.

Assyrian military supremacy depended on the accuracy of its infantry bowmen who were supported by cavalry with bow and javelin. No state could stand against them until the Medes, mounted on their locally bred Nisean horses, made cavalry their main aim. The horse, traditionally used by the Persians when riding and hunting, brought them into formerly inaccessible areas of the empire and changed the entire concept of warfare. The cavalry formed an intensive and indispensable part of Achaemenian war tactics, especially when horsemen with bow and javelin were capable of destroying the enemy from a distance. Until saddles and stirrups came into use, however, there were serious difficulties for a mounted bowman who needed both hands free for shooting. Even the Persian kings were not immune to falling from their mounts. The war chariot, driven by one man, allowing another freedom to shoot, partly solved this problem. Though expert horsemen, the Persians, when forced to fight without cavalry or when the terrain neutralised the value of mounted troops, were no match for Greek hoplites or other armoured pikemen. The humiliating wars with Greece convinced Xerxes and his successors of the need for military reorganisation. Instead of reconstructing their own army, however, the later Persians followed the unimaginative and dangerous course of hiring mercenaries—10,000 Greeks alone were estimated to be in Achaemenian service. The Persians nevertheless remained a powerful military force until they were outclassed, both in the arts of war and in organisation, by Macedonia.

# 5

# *How They Travelled*

BEFORE the Achaemenians, the majority of roads throughout the Middle East had been little more than caravan trails between one centre of civilised life and another. They spanned vast wildernesses infested with thieves and marauders, and well-armed escorts were needed to accompany travellers, particularly merchants. Iran was crossed by a number of time-honoured trade routes which linked the Indian sub-continent and the Far East with the Mediterranean seaboard, chiefly the Levantine ports of Syria. Skirting the northern edge of the Dasht-i-Kavir and the southern shore of the Caspian was the great silk route to China. Coming from Ctesiphon—near modern Baghdad—on the eastern bank of the Tigris, it headed for the Iranian plateau through modern Kermanshah, Hamadan and Tehran. Circumventing the Kavir, the route passed to Herat in Afghanistan before branching north-eastwards to Merv (Mary), Bukhara, Samarkand and on to China, or turning southwards to Seistan, east to Quandahar and over the Baluchistan mountains to the Indus plains. Another important branch route passed through the Elburz Mountains, near Tehran, by way of the famous Caspian Gates where later, at its narrowest part, the Persians erected iron gates and stationed guards. The counterpart of the great northern route was one which from Isfahan, Yazd and Kerman skirted the south-eastern edge of the Dasht-i-Lut with projections eastwards to the Indus and westwards to the Mesopotamian lowlands at Susa. Both these trans-continental arteries were linked by a transverse route from the Persian Gulf port of Bushire to Shiraz and Isfahan, proceeding north-westwards to Hamadan, Tabriz in Azerbaijan, Armenia and on to the Black or Caspian Seas.

The development of the Persian road network from these older lines of communication was probably initiated by Cyrus, but its organisation owed much to Darius, especially when the system was progressively extended to serve new conquests in the east. Though little accurate detail is known, the Achaemenian network of highways and posting stations linking provincial centres with the royal authority seems to have been extensive and intelligently planned, since it survived the empire for many centuries. Both Susa and Ecbatana were destined to become major centres on the new network. The road to Bactria and India is referred to by Ctesias in the last part of his Persian history; but much of the information on the road system comes from Herodotus and, to a lesser extent, Xenophon. Both refer to the imperial highways, particularly the Royal Road which ran from Ephesus and Sardis on the Aegean coast of Asia Minor to Susa, where it was extended to Persepolis. Trade was obviously stimulated by the improvements in transport and, after about 448 BC, commerce and communications appear to have been so unhindered that Herodotus could travel anywhere at will within the Persian world.

THE ROYAL ROAD

Covering a distance of over 1,670 miles (2,672km) the Royal Road was the lifeline of the empire and hence the most heavily travelled of the Persian highways. Parts of the road between northern Mesopotamia and Cappadocia had originally been opened up as early as the third millennium BC by Assyrian pioneer traders whose settlements in Cappadocia had subsequently been embraced by Akkad and Sumer. Its extension and elaboration was the work of the Achaemenian kings, though the detailed alignment of certain sections of the highway has long been a matter of debate. Some points at issue, especially with regard to the places where the highway crossed the rivers Tigris, Euphrates and their tributaries, have been clarified by Victor W. von Hagen, leader of the Persian Royal Road Expedition which set out in May 1974 after a series of preliminary studies. Working with scant evidence, it tracked the course of the highway from Susa to the Aegean (Figure 6).

Out of Susa the Royal Road traversed the eastern edge of the Mesopotamian plain, intersecting with the Babylon-Ecbatana road, then crossed the Diyala, a tributary of the Tigris, before proceeding to modern Kirkuk. Over the Little Zab, the road went on to Irbil, crossing both the Great Zab and the Tigris a little above Mosul in the vicinity of ancient Nineveh. From Nineveh the Royal Road followed the Tigris to Dyarbakir and then passed over the Euphrates at the Tomissa crossing—later to become famous in Rome's wars with the Parthians, the neo-Persian state which had risen out of the *dejecta membra* of the Achaemenian empire. From Tomissa (modern Izolu) the route tackled the Anti-Taurus mountains between Matatya and Kayseri and then followed an earlier alignment to the old Hittite capital of Hattusas (modern Bagazkale) and on to Ankara, Afyon and Dinar, before descending from the Asia Minor plateau to Sardis and the Aegean coast.

Caravans took an estimated ninety days to travel from Susa to Sardis. The route was measured in *parasangs* which, strictly speaking, were measures of time rather than of distance; *sang*, meaning a stone, must have referred to some visual method of indicating the stage reached in the journey. On flat terrain the Persian planners estimated a day's journey to be about five parasangs—perhaps 18 miles (28km)—whereas in more difficult country the parasangs referred to smaller distances. The *strathmoi* of Seleucid times were probably based on the Achaemenian system of route measurement; this, according to Frye, is still observable in parts of Persia, and in Afghanistan where it refers to the distance a horse can travel in an hour.

For the convenience of travellers, staging-posts and official inns or resting places were maintained along the entire route, their frequency depending on the nature of the terrain and

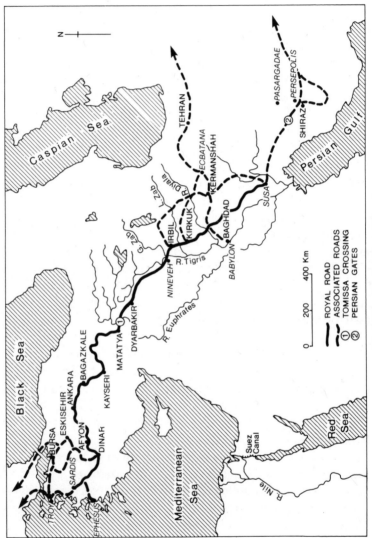

Fig 6 The Persian Royal Road

physical conditions in general. Along the route through Armenia, for example, there were fifteen stages or posting-stations in a distance of just over 52 parasangs. There is no evidence that inns were set up on the other major arteries, but the route to Egypt, via Sinai, had water caches along its desert stretches. Water, in earthenware jugs formerly holding Greek and Phoenician wine, was stored underground at regular intervals. This, however, may have been for military expediency, as indeed were the heavily guarded check-points along the imperial highways. To protect it from bandits and marauders, the Royal Road had two check-points on the borders of Cicilia, with another one in Armenia and one on the Halys river. The latter functioned as a type of passport control for, states Herodotus, 'the bridge over the river had gates through which everyone must pass and a military post nearby'. Large rivers, crossed by pontoon bridges or ferries, were protected by guard-posts, as were all provincial boundaries where traffic was subject to searching.

The Royal Road was a cleared track rather than a metalled highway in the Roman or modern sense. This seems to have been characteristic of the early Persian roads, though a method was developed of paving parts of the road in areas of soft subsoil and even of making artificial ruts for wheeled transport. All the main Persian roads were in good enough condition to permit the rapid passage of messengers and large armies accompanied by carriages, waggons and chariots. The earliest examples of wheeled vehicles, came from a broad area centred on Lakes Van and Urmia, though their invention was related to early farming communities pre-dating by many centuries the arrival of the Persians. The latter, however, made great use of wheeled transport, especially light-wheeled chariots for warfare, hunting and racing. A miniature gold model—part of the Oxus Treasure—shows the passenger sitting with his back to the driver, who stood while controlling the four-horse team. Though the iron horse-shoe was not introduced until the second or first centuries BC, protective shoes were made of copper, leather and horsehair. For both military and commercial travel, pack animals and ox-drawn carts were used.

## SECONDARY ROADS

A system of secondary roads and trackways complemented the broad imperial highways, though in the mountainous and more isolated parts of the empire they were hardly better than rough footpaths for pedestrian and pack-animal traffic. The secondary route system appears best developed in western Asia Minor around Sardis, in Mesopotamia east of the Tigris and in Parsa. Many of these roads, especially the one connecting Susa with Persepolis, were built to facilitate the journeys of the royal court. At Jin Jin, near Fahlian in the Zagros foothills, are the remains of a royal pavilion where the kings stopped for refreshment. Near a broad river in wooded country, the site was an ideal halting place to break a journey of several days before beginning the long ascent to the plateau by way of the 'Persian Gates'. Another road, through Luristan, linked Susa with Ecbatana.

## THE COURIER SERVICE

The famous system of post-roads and professional messengers was not a Persian innovation but the development of a form of governmental machinery already practised in Assyria, Babylonia and Egypt. It appears that in Babylonia there were four or five classes of messengers, though it is not clear exactly how they differed or were classified. In Persia the normal method of communication between central government and provinces was by officials—the king's messengers—who made swift journeys on horseback, conveying imperial commands and despatches. 'There is nothing mortal that goes faster than these messengers,' Herodotus says, 'so well have the Persians organised the matter. They say that at every day's journey along the whole route there are horses and men stationed, whom neither snow, nor rain, nor heat, nor darkness checks from completing their allotted course at the utmost speed. One galloper passes the message to another, and he to a third, and so on, as in the torch-races which the Greeks run in honour of the Fire-God.' Whereas it took caravans ninety days, the couriers covered the route from Susa to Sardis in a week. Messages were sometimes inscribed on tablets, but a more convenient method was an Aramaic inscription written in ink on papyrus, parchment or hide.

The post-roads also served the purposes of espionage and kept the government informed about its subjects. Private correspondence passing along the roads was carefully examined and liable to confiscation or censorship. Individuals wishing to maintain the privacy of their communications and escape the vigilance of officials were forced to resort to ruses such as that described by Herodotus. The only safe way that Histiaeus could think of sending a message of revolt to Aristagoras was by marking the scalp of his trustiest slave. The head was shaved and the message pricked on to the skin. When the slave's hair grew again he was dispatched from Susa to Miletus with the instruction 'bid Aristagoras shave your head and look thereon'.

The Persian courier service was complemented by a primitive, though efficient, form of signals communication, which transmitted messages rapidly from hilltop fire towers. The system remained in operation in Iran until the telegraph made it obsolete in the nineteenth century.

### WATER TRANSPORT

Iran proper possesses few important rivers and those it has are of little use for navigation because of their strength in the wet season and their intermittent character for the remainder of the year. The great river systems of the Middle East—the Tigris–Euphrates, the Nile and the Indus—all fell within the Achaemenian empire, however, and their navigability was vital to the movement of goods and basic to commercial and administrative control. Persia's annexation of the Indus basin was a historical event of greatest importance. For many centuries, certainly since the times of the Aryan invasion, the civilisations of the Indus had fallen into decadence, and the river had ceased to be used for navigation purposes. Darius' economic policy was clearly aimed at establishing a link between the economies of the Mediterranean, Central Asia and the Far East, and restoration of the economic life of the Punjab was a necessary first step in this ideal. Scylax's voyage of discovery (see page 79) was part and parcel of Darius' wider plans.

The Nile and the Mesopotamian rivers, on the other hand, were navigable, much as they are today. Boats could sail the Nile as far as the First Cataract—that is, near Aswan—and, according to Strabo and other sources, the Tigris was navigable to Opis, the Euphrates to Babylon, and the Eulaeus to Susa. Opis and Babylon were more than 3,000 stadia—about 350 miles (563km)—distant from the Shatt-al-Arab, the delta mouth of the Tigris-Euphrates. Both rivers must have presented a busy scene, for there are references to the 'sailors of Opis' and to the Euphrates port of Mari being an important boat-building centre. Upstream, rafts laden with merchandise were floated down the Tigris from Nineveh and Assur to Opis. The skins which held the rafts together were transported back by pack animals, whereas the wood used in their construction was sold at the destination port. It is highly likely that the building materials for the palace at Susa and other Achaemenian works were transported along the Mesopotamian rivers. Wood from Lebanon and the Levant in general was dragged overland to suitable points on the river to be floated as rafts. The transport of large quantities of stone, metal, gypsum, marble and asphalt was also dependent on the rivers.

### SEA NAVIGATION

Rivergoing vessels plied the seas between the Persian Gulf, the Levant and Egypt, and this necessitated the long voyage around Arabia. The Persians were not a maritime people, perhaps because their original homeland offered little inducement to sea navigation—the coast of Fars is poor in harbours and its approach rendered difficult by shallows and rocks. The maritime plain, with its stifling heat, infertile soil and turbulent mountain torrents in the rainy season, is ill-suited to maintain a considerable population and acts as a further isolating factor. That the early kings took an interest in the Persian Gulf is substantiated, however, by the discovery of a palace, attributable to Cyrus the Great, near Bushire. It is also somewhat surprising that the most far-reaching and ambitious of all Darius' projects was his attempt to foster the commercial use of the southern seas and, in particular, to increase traffic in the Indian Ocean. This was attempted through voyages of discovery, the completion of the Suez Canal, and the construction of harbours and moorings on the Persian Gulf.

Persian ships were manned by Carians, Phoenicians, Greeks, Syrians, Cretans and Milesians. Around 500 BC, exiled Milesians were settled at the mouth of the Shatt-al-Arab to organise navigation on the rivers and in the Persian Gulf. Carian sailors, in particular, have left their traces in the graffiti at Abydus, Abu Simbel and Wadi Halfa, and, as the *Shipbuilding Papyrus* reveals, there was an international crowd of seafaring people in Egypt under Persian rule. Already ship's papers were in use and sailors were graded in accordance with their skills. The expansion of trade, however, led to further institutions such as trading pacts, international law and blockading.

Modelled on Greek and Phoenician craft, Persian ships were propelled by a single square sail. New vessels of greater length and beam than anything previously designed were built to accommodate the first long-distance maritime trade in bulk goods. These craft, capable of sailing 60 to 80 miles in a day, could transport over 200 tons of freight by sea and more than 100 tons by normal navigation on the great rivers. Such vessels, together with improved roads and the old caravan trails, turned the Persian empire into an early 'common market'.

THE SUEZ CANAL

A canal linking the Red Sea with the Mediterranean was of fundamental importance to Darius' objectives. Herodotus attributes work on the first canal to Pharaoh Necho, but it was originally dug by Seti I of the Nineteenth dynasty in the fourteenth century BC. Necho resolved to make himself master of the Indian trade route by using the canal as a major waterway from the Red Sea near Bubastis through Lake Timsah and the Wadi Tumilat to the Mediterranean. Darius, who may have passed through the Wadi on his way to Egypt, found that the canal was dry for 85 miles (136km) of its length. He undertook to complete the project from the Gulf of Suez to a point where it joined the Pelusiac branch of the Nile and hence connected with the Mediterranean.

Darius' artificial watercourse was 150ft (45m) wide and more than 90 miles (144km) long; including the natural waterway through the Bitter Lakes, the entire canal extended 125 miles (200km). It was probably opened around 500 BC. A series of massive granite stelae were erected along its banks, one of which was discovered by de Lesseps in 1866 during construction of the modern canal. The text on the stele leaves no doubt that the project was of personal interest to Darius: 'I ordered this canal to be built from the Nile, Pirava, which flows in Egypt, into the sea that goes to Parsa: it [was built] as I had ordered and [ships] sailed from Egypt through the canal into Parsa, as was my kama [pleasure].' In the Egyptian text, twenty-four ships with tribute for Persia are recorded as inaugurating the canal.

The Suez Canal was perhaps the greatest achievement of Darius' reign, for it epitomised his vast design of uniting Egypt, Mesopotamia and India into a single economic system. Mesopotamia, in fact, lost something of its importance as the great trade route to the East, and Egypt was called upon to play the role which had until then brought prosperity to the Tigris-

Euphrates lowlands. With the opening of the canal, India became part of the economic life of the West, though it was not
until the time of Alexander the Great that the entire sea route
gained international importance. By the fourth century BC,
Egypt had regained its independence and the Persian empire
lost the use of the canal, which fell into disuse and decay. Subsequent attempts to repair it were made by Ptolemy Philadelphus
and the Emperor Trajan, and the canal lasted to the eighth
century AD.

## VOYAGES OF DISCOVERY

Darius' sponsorship of exploratory sea voyages was part of his
ambitious project for making Persia a major sea power by linking the eastern marches of the empire to its western possessions.
Exploration followed upon conquest, and the Persians were the
first to secure accurate information about the Nile south of
Egypt. Cambyses, after successfully subduing the Ethiopians
beyond the First Cataract, planned three further campaigns:
one by sea against Carthage, of which nothing is known;
another with infantry against the Saharan oasis of Siwa, in
which at el-Khargeh, seven days out of Thebes, his army was
destroyed in a sandstorm; and a third, far south of Egypt,
against the Ethiopians who were believed to dwell on the
shores of the Southern Ocean. The Persian interest in Egypt
is also reflected in the voyage of Scylax, though initially his
commission was to explore the navigability of the Indus and
Indian Ocean before surveying the way to Egypt. His report,
a sailor's log-book, was dedicated to Darius and some passages of the Indus voyage have been preserved in Herodotus
and other authors.

Scylax, a Greek of Asia Minor from the town of Caryanda
and one of the greatest Carian navigators, was admiral of the
Persian fleet under Cambyses and Darius. The date of his
voyage is not known and its duration of thirty months,
quoted by Herodotus, is probably an over-estimation. It was

apparently undertaken shortly after the conquest of north-west India (the Punjab) rather than as part of the initial preparation for augmenting this territory. The fact that Scylax mentions a Persian garrison on the 'Indus' river seems to support this, though it is not clear which river Scylax navigated. His voyage was from east to west and he apparently reached India by an overland route. He presumably sailed down either the Kabul or the Indus, but certainly not the Ganges, as some early scholars have suggested. From the east, he seems to have found his way around Arabia to the Red Sea and finally arrived in the neighbourhood of Suez.

Though largely preoccupied with the southern seas and oceans, Darius also took steps to inform himself more accurately about the inhabitants and general political situation of the Mediterranean. Information had already reached the empire via the Greeks, Phoenicians and other maritime peoples, but the Greeks were adept at concealing news which might be useful to commercial competitors. Following the conquest of the Asia Minor city-states, local inhabitants were required to act as guides to Persian officers, who brought back reliable reports. According to Herodotus, Democedes of Croton, a doctor who had been reduced to a Persian slave, was commissioned by Darius to guide an expedition in the Mediterranean. Democedes later escaped, but the Persian officers accompanying him undertook a leisurely reconnaissance of Greece before proceeding to Italy.

Darius bequeathed something of his sea-sense to Xerxes, who sent Sataspes to circumnavigate Africa from Gibraltar to Egypt via the Atlantic Ocean. Herodotus, who obviously relished this titbit of Persian scandal, says that Sataspes—an Achaemenian noble of royal blood (perhaps a cousin of Xerxes)—was condemned to death for an offence against one of the ladies of the court. Through the intercession of his mother, Xerxes' aunt, his sentence was commuted to sailing around Africa—probably after 478 or 470 BC.

Sataspes' ship had been fitted out in Egypt and was no doubt manned by Egyptians, Phoenicians or Greeks. Sailing through the Pillars, he hugged the shores of Morocco, the Sahara desert and Senegal, and may have reached the western end of the Gulf of Guinea. Sataspes then appears to have turned back—possibly as a result of the Doldrums, or because of the Canary Current and the south-west trade winds which blow in summer. Certainly this voyage was unsuccessful, though he returned with plausible stories of the Negrito peoples, later to be confirmed by other west African voyages. Xerxes, disbelieving him, had Sataspes impaled.

The Achaemenian voyages of discovery, aided by the introduction of coinage (see Chapter 6), meant that maritime as well as overland trade was extended to far-distant countries. Under Xerxes and later monarchs, Greek, Phoenician and other mariners maintained connections between the Indian Ocean, the Persian Gulf, Mesopotamia, the Nile and Mediterranean ports. World commerce spread as far west as the Danube and the Rhine. The discovery of jars, in which oil, spices and drugs were transported, provide evidence of further commercial links between Iran, India and Ceylon.

# 6

# *How They Worked*

PERSIA's unprecedented prosperity under Darius was related to a number of co-ordinated development programmes which affected almost every aspect of national life. Herodotus' description of Darius as 'a merchant' or 'shopkeeper' must certainly be taken as a compliment and tribute to the king's ability to create the healthy economy that came to be regarded as one of the pillars of his reign.

While the political unification of the whole of western Asia and its division into satrapies under central control were the initial and essential steps towards achieving a national economy, there were other equally powerful factors that gave it impetus. The creation of protected land and sea routes linking its different parts, a balanced system of tax collection, the standardisation of weights and measures and, above all, the introduction, or perfection, of a system of coinage, collectively stimulated commerce whose volume in the sixth and fifth centuries BC surpassed anything previously known in the ancient world. Under Darius the resources of the empire were canalised into an elaborate economic system in which the king was technically the sole proprietor of a vast profit-making enterprise.

### COINAGE

While the use of precious metals as a basis of sale and exchange was familiar from early times in the Middle East, there was no standardised system of coinage. Terms such as *talent* and *shekel* referred to weight and were commonly used as a measure of value, usually in silver, by which to adjust barter transactions. As a means of exchange this caused problems for a scale was needed to determine the value of the sum changing hands and also a test of purity had to be made when the integrity of the metal was in doubt. Much expertise, time and equipment was required to conclude an honest deal.

Croesus of Lydia is traditionally credited with the invention and introduction of a stamped, officially guaranteed coinage as a medium of exchange on a state scale, though almost certainly several other commercially important Greek trading cities, including Miletus, Aegina and Corinth, took similar revolutionary steps. Darius is traditionally given credit for introducing Persian coinage, but it is debatable whether the *daric*, the principal unit of the imperial currency, was named after him or stemmed from the old word *dari*, meaning gold. Though the coinage of Persia is confessedly modelled on that of Lydia, it is difficult to believe that, during the time between the conquest of Lydia and the reforms of Darius, coins were not issued by Cyrus and Cambyses to take the place of Lydian money. The Persian governors of Sardis may have continued to issue money of the types and standard of Croesus; alternatively, the *daric* could have been coined immediately after the conquest, by Cyrus rather than Darius. Almost certainly Darius perfected the monetary system; the purity of his coinage is confirmed by Herodotus, but he does not imply that Darius introduced it.

The Persian gold daric is undoubtedly one of the most famous coins of the ancient world. It bears a representation of the king kneeling, or perhaps running, holding spear and bow, and wearing the royal tiara. The reverse is an oblong incuse. In weight the Persian gold coinage was superior to the Lydian, but its metallic content, following the Babylonian standard, was a little less pure. The daric, $\frac{3}{4}$in (19mm) in diameter, weighed $\frac{1}{3}$oz (9.5g) and was 98-per-cent pure gold; the remaining 2 per cent was an alloy of silver and other metals to harden the coin. Minting gold coins was the exclusive prerogative of the throne, a privilege jealously guarded and enforced. Any unauthorised minting of gold coins was regarded as a sign of rebellion and carried the death penalty. Another stabilising factor in the currency system was the close supervision of the royal mint to ensure that coins conformed in shape and metallic content.

Silver coinage, the *sigloi*, which supplemented the daric, was 90-per-cent pure silver and 10-per-cent alloy. Twenty sigloi equalled one daric. Silver and copper coins could be minted and circulated by the Persian viceroys, chiefly for payment of military service. The kings, with characteristic liberality, also permitted the semi-autonomous Greek and Phoenician states the privilege of issuing silver coinage. Official exchange rates were established between Greek silver coins, of regular weight and composition, and Persian gold. The independent minting of silver currency, especially in outlying satrapies, led to considerable abuse by the imperial tax collectors. They usually ignored the face value of all but the royal sigloi, accepting those minted elsewhere only by weight, and often discounting them unfairly. Such measures prevented the debasement of royal coinage, but subsequently led to trouble and revolts.

Persian gold currency inundated the whole Greek world; undoubtedly later coins were struck from their metal, particularly those of Alexander the Great. The silver sigloi also circulated widely and in immense quantities. A large proportion of these bear countermarks, probably stamped on them by the imperial tax collectors or by local authorities, as a guarantee of their worth in particular districts.

Stairway reliefs of the Tripylon, Persepolis. Median nobles carrying lilies walk in procession to the banquet hall. In order to maintain a uniform level of heads the sculptor has interposed dwarf figures to counteract the elevation of the steps

A relief from the Persepolis Treasury. Darius is shown giving audience before two fire altars and an usher introduces the delegation. The Crown Prince, Xerxes, stands behind with his hand on the throne, the conventional way of depicting the right of succession

A universal currency, together with protected trade routes, meant that commerce, though initially developing more rapidly within the empire, could expand internationally. For Darius, however, the coinage had great potential for propaganda purposes and the setting up of a financial administrative network, independent of the satrapies, greatly curbed provincial power.

### THE LAND

The basis of Achaemenian wealth and the key to the national economy was land. Theoretically, all of it belonged to the king but in practice it was divided into direct royal lands—which included estates, mines and forests—and the major category of what may be called 'feudal' land—that occupied by local rulers or tribes, over whom the king had nominal control, and large estates held in fief from the king. Royal grants of land were commonly given in proportion to the military obligations of his subjects. Feudalism was also promoted by establishing colonies of soldiers in conquered lands—mainly in Egypt and Asia Minor. Fiefs were grouped into larger 'cantons' which acted as tax collecting districts; as the money economy grew, feudal monetary dues replaced the former military obligations. In many parts of the empire, chiefly in Babylonia, extensive lands were held by temples, with the high priest acting as tax collector for the royal treasury. There were probably land holdings of all types within the boundaries of a satrapy.

While privately owned smallholdings existed, especially in Parsa, Achaemenian agriculture, and other forms of land exploitation, was based on the large estates. These were worked by an army of peasants and serfs who produced everything

Twenty-two miles (thirty-five kilometres) east of Kermanshah is the rock face of Behistun which carries the bas-relief commemorating Darius the Great's triumph over the upstart kings. Carved at a height of 200ft (60m), its trilingual inscription in Old Persian, Akkadian and Elamite was deciphered by Colonel Rawlinson in 1847 required by the owner. In strict feudal fashion, these labourers were probably forbidden to leave their domicile without the permission of the landlord or satrapy official. Absentee ownership, the traditional scourge of the Middle East, seems to have been a characteristic of the Achaemenian estates. Persian noblemen, particularly in isolated satrapies, were reluctant to spend much time in local residence, prefering the attractions of the cities and royal courts. Superintendents or estate managers were left in charge of their land, but such a system led to local discontent and ultimately undermined the stability of provincial government. Aramaic papyri from Egypt give a graphic account of the estates of Arsames, royal prince and governor of Egypt, who spent much of his time in Susa or Babylon, whilst agents managed his lands. The large estate owned by an urban resident is a characteristic of Persian agricultural land which has survived into this century.


### WATER AND IRRIGATION

Whereas land was the chief source of Achaemenian wealth, water was the major key to its life and successful exploitation. Persia proper is not watered by rivers like the Nile, Tigris and Euphrates, nor does it enjoy a regular rainfall regime beneficial to agriculture. From earliest times irrigation was essential to the maintenance of most forms of agriculture; the distribution and intensity of human activity reflected the availability of water, either on the surface or beneath the soil within reach of constantly improving technology. As dry farming was practicable only in the north-western region, the Achaemenians developed their own methods of irrigation, as well as elaborating and perfecting the systems of conquered lands. Persia's most glorious days were inaugurated by achievements in water control that were exceptionally advanced for the period and the empire's decline resulted as much from water mismanagement as from the more easily understood political and physical disasters brought about by later conquests. According to

Polybius, the Achaemenians 'granted the enjoyment of the profits of the lands to the inhabitants of some of the waterless districts for five generations on the conditions of their bringing fresh water in'.

Water management under the Achaemenians received a great deal of attention. In Babylonia, for example, the irrigation canals of the Tigris and Euphrates, and their tributaries, were greatly extended and the satrapy's agricultural potential was consequently increased. Similar improvements were made to the ancient dams and canals of Elam, though the supply of water from the Karun and Karkheh was less reliable owing to seasonal and erratic rainfall. On the plateau, the rugged terrain, enclosed valleys and the absence of large streams prevented the development of an extensive and integrated irrigation network. Open canals, which tapped streams, springs and wells, brought water from considerable distances to settlements and fields. The mechanical lifts for raising water were probably those traditionally associated with the Middle East, including the counter-weighted lever with skin bucket and animal hoist with hide bucket, and various kinds of water-wheel.

The ancient Persians adopted, and perfected, a remarkable system of underground canals known today as *qanats* in western Iran and *kariz* in the east; also as *foggara* and *falaj* elsewhere in the Middle East. In Achaemenian times, qanats were found throughout the plateau; Polybius particularly mentions the large number in Media. Based on the gravity-feed system, a qanat consists of a slightly inclined tunnel, often several kilometres in length, which taps a reliable water source (Figure 7). The slope of the tunnel is less than that of the ground surface, so that water is discharged where the two slopes meet. Once a water supply is located, a mother-well is sunk to below the level of the water table and, at regular intervals above and downslope of this, other shafts are built whose bottoms are connected to form the conduit. These shafts also ventilate the tunnel and provide access for builders and repairers. Lateral tunnels may also tap other water-bearing strata. Emerging at

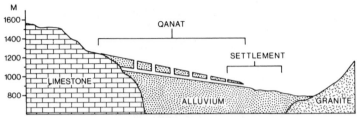

Fig 7 A generalised diagram of a qanat

the surface, the water is usually led to a small reservoir where its flow is controlled to supply the needs of the settlement and its fields.

This tunnel system was probably first developed by the Urartians for mining purposes, but it was the Persians who perfected it for the transportation of water. The qanat became an accepted method of irrigation throughout the dry areas of the empire and was subsequently adopted in Central Asia, Arabia, the Sahara and the Mediterranean world.

## AGRICULTURE

The Persian empire was greatly dependent on the agricultural production of its varied provinces. Fars, in the fifth and fourth centuries BC, was a flourishing region, which produced barley, wheat, vines and olives, and raised cattle, sheep and goats, together with draught animals. Media, its nearest neighbour, also combined cultivation with a developed grazing industry—cattle and horses—but showed closer analogies with more northerly satrapies where Mesopotamian influence was less felt. It was Babylonia, however, with its rich soil and integrated irrigation system, that was the garden of the empire. 'The blades of wheat and barley are at least three inches wide,' says Herodotus, 'as for millet and sesame, I will not say to what astonishing size they grow, though I know well enough.' This was a clever literary way of emphasizing his point, 'for I know that people', he continues, 'who have not been to Babylonia have refused to believe even what I have already said about its fertility.' The date palm, another source of Babylonian wealth, was taxed twice as much as grain—for not only did the palm provide food, wine and honey but also raw materials for construction, rope-making and basketry. Other productive regions based on rich soils and irrigation were the satrapies along the Oxus river whose agricultural wealth vied with Mesopotamia and earned for them the title of 'Babylonia of the East'.

In contrast to the settled farmers, there were groups of nomadic and semi-nomadic pastoralists, consisting of both Iranian and pre-Iranian tribes. Their primitive existence revolved around the breeding and herding of cattle and sheep, and they probably supplied skins, wool and other animal products.

*Crop Cultivation*

The character of agriculture in the vast Persian empire obviously varied with environmental conditions. As a deliberate policy, the Achaemenians, took a personal interest in the introduction and propagation of new crops. The cultural and physical barriers, which formerly separated Asian agriculture into its Middle Eastern, Indian and Far Eastern branches, were broken down, and exotic seeds and saplings were despatched to satrapies for experimental cultivation. Agricultural improvements were rewarded with grants of land and other gifts. Darius, in particular, commended all such innovations. In a curious letter, Darius orders Gadatas, an Ionian official, to transplant trees and other species from the east into Asia Minor and Syria. He ends by praising Gadatas for 'improving my country with fruit trees from the other side of the Euphrates'.

In Damascus the Persians attempted to cultivate a type of vine that was highly esteemed at their court. They also introduced pistachios in Aleppo, which later spread throughout Asia Minor and Greece. Other crop introductions included sesame into Egypt, and rice and flax into Mesopotamia, flax being grown as a cloth fibre rather than as an oil plant. One of

the most important crops to spread abroad was alfalfa or
lucerne, known to the Greeks as Medish grass (Medicago).
This grew prolifically in the valleys of Media and was spread to
Greece as a result of being used as feed for Persian army horses
on active service there.

LIVESTOCK

Animal husbandry, a specific virtue in the traditional Aryan
religion, was especially important to the empire's well-being. The
Persians brought the strong riding horses of the Medes into use
throughout their territories and beyond into Europe, India,
China and Arabia. Median horses had long been the coveted
prizes of Middle Eastern empires, particularly Assyria. In 843
BC Salmanassar III carried off from Nawar 'numberless horses
broken to the yoke', and in 714 BC Sargon received 4,609 horses,
together with mules and other tributes, from the forty-five
chiefs of the 'country of the mighty Medes'. The Nisean horses,
named after a Median plain, were the most famous breed on
account of their taller and heavier stature, and are
frequently mentioned in classical writings. The Persepolis
reliefs indicate that Armenia, Cappadocia, Syria and Scy-
thia were other important horse-breeding provinces.

The Persians played a vital role in the domestication of
the camel. It was Cyrus who initially used it in warfare
against the Lydians; presumably this was the Bactrian
variety. The Arabian camel, which had been domesticated centuries earlier by people on the caravan route between Yemen
and Midia was utilised by Cambyses. As a beast of burden
the camel spread to most parts of the Middle East and
North Africa. Invariably it was followed, or accompanied, by
the sheep and goat. The Persians were also responsible for
the introduction to the west of the domestic fowl, the white
dove and the peacock—all natives of Asia.

Hunting and fishing remained important pursuits
throughout the empire, supplementing food supplies for a

large section of the population as well as providing sport for the aristocracy. The fisheries of the Persian Gulf, the Tigris and the Euphrates exported salted, dried and cured fish in jars. Herodotus mentions that part of Egypt's imperial tribute consisted of profits from its fisheries.

### FORESTRY AND MINERALS

Being interested in the propagation of plants, the Persians were naturally concerned with the vital question of forest exploitation, for which there appears to have been some measure of planning. The Sumerian princes drew supplies of timber from the Zagros, which was also extensively exploited by the Achaemenians for the construction of palaces, boats, chariots, carts, implements and machines of war. There were timbers, such as teak from India and cedar from Lebanon; other regions active in the timber trade were Asia Minor, Crete and Cyprus.

Mining and quarrying were important activities. From earliest times the quarries of the plateau and its surrounding mountains had provided marble, alabaster and building stone for the Mesopotamian civilisations, but the greatest demand came from the Achaemenian construction projects. Metals and precious stones were exploited from an early period. Iron, copper, tin and lead attracted the attention of the conquering Assyrians. Copper also came from Palestine, Lebanon and Cyprus; iron from Lebanon, the Caucasus and the upper Tigris and Euphrates valleys, and tin from Seistan and Cyprus.

In Iran proper, gold and silver were mined in the Kerman region. Silver was also brought from Palestine, the southern shores of the Black Sea and Egypt. Gold was obtained from the eastern satrapies and from Sardis, which controlled the Greek mines of Thasos and Pactolis. The gold resources of the eastern steppes, which had initially been exploited by the Scythians, were under the control of Bactria.

CRAFTS AND INDUSTRY

The presence of varied raw materials, the expansion of international commerce, and the numbers of rich patrons attached to the courts of kings and satraps encouraged craftsmanship and manufacturing industry in general. The courts set the fashion in dress, jewellery and household items, and local artists and artisans, adjusting their traditional skills and styles to the new taste in luxury goods (see Chapter 7), acquired well-deserved reputations. Goldsmiths and silversmiths in particular developed metallurgical techniques, as well as fusing a number of artistic traditions into a composite Achaemenian style. The renowned 'Treasure of Oxus', discovered on the banks of the Oxus in 1877, provides a microcosm of Achaemenian craftsmanship in gold and silver. Now in the British Museum and the Victoria and Albert Museum, these objects may have come from a cache of precious goods hidden at some troubled time, or perhaps represent the accumulated wealth of offerings made to a temple or shrine. Some of the finest artisans were in Babylonia; their tradition and expertise in enamelled terracottas were utilised to full advantage in the glazed-brick friezes decorating the palace of Susa. Several of these—reconstructed by French archaeologists from fragments found at the site—are now in the Louvre.

Manufacturing was not solely directed to the production of luxury goods for the aristocracy. Increasingly, all classes of people were provided for, and the marketing of cheaper cotton and woollen garments, leather goods, particularly footwear, and household items began to centre on the towns and cities. Workshops based on artisan-serf labour, however, continued to thrive on the large estates.

THE LABOUR FORCE

The cosmopolitan and co-operative nature of Achaemenian rule is reflected in the skilled workers employed on the great building projects. These working forces came from all quarters of the empire and labour exchanges may well have existed to deal with their recruitment and to organise some form of worker legislation. Certainly there was considerable mobilisation of labour and talent, as revealed in the Susa Foundation Charter which refers to Ionian and Sardian stone-cutters, Median and Egyptian goldsmiths and wall decorators, and Babylonian brick-makers. At Persepolis isolated texts speak of Carian goldsmiths, Egyptian wood-carvers and inscription-makers, and Syrian and Ionian labourers. Babylonian tablets, which made no mention of Persian names before 521 BC, thereafter list them in ever-increasing numbers among those mobilised for labour and services. The majority, however, as in other satrapies, were officials—governors, administrators, judges and tax-collectors.

The Persepolis Treasury Tablets provide interesting information on regulations concerning work, wages and modes of payment. The Achaemenians apparently took an active interest in its labour force—at any rate those employed on imperial projects. The majority of these tablets were, in effect, pay sheets for the building of the palace; it is evident that wages for different classes of workers—skilled and unskilled, women and children—were strictly controlled. Monetary payments were pitifully small, with treasury accountants receiving the equivalent of 6 or 8 shekels a month and the treasury labourer about $\frac{1}{12}$ shekel. These small accounts of cash, however, were merely a portion of the total remuneration, being supplements to real wages paid in kind, perhaps as sheep, wine, beer or grain. Wine, a particularly common part of the pay packet, was equivalent in value to 1 shekel, while a sheep was rated at 3 shekels. For certain treasury workers there were employment 'perks' in the form of daily rations from the court kitchens—the Great King fed as many as 15,000 persons daily.

Whether the treasury tablets provide a picture of the transitional period that followed the introduction of coinage is a debatable question. Previously payment of wages had been entirely in kind. Even by the time of Xerxes, two-thirds were paid in kind, and subsequently this was reduced to one-third. According to G. G. Cameron, the treasury pay sheets consisted of two documents or tablets which were attached to each other with a cord; one stipulated the portion of wages owing an employee to be paid in kind, and the other gave the balance of pay, granted in coined money. These documents might support the brief comments of the unknown author in Aristotle's *Oeconomica* which relate how the Achaemenian kings regulated expenses. The royal budget was balanced by a determination of when expenses were paid and how much were paid in kind or in coined money. By careful manipulation of wage payments, the treasury was able to reap considerable profits.

### BANKS AND CREDIT

The administration of royal and temple treasuries provided a primitive system of banking which, particularly in Babylonia, was supplemented by professional private banks stimulated by the new fiscal organisation. The bankers were wealthy merchants who handled other people's money for profit and their financial influence entered every branch of the economy. Absentee landlords and distant estates necessitated the transportation of money and goods, and this provided the main business of the banking houses. They advanced loans, a man's estate, his slaves and other possessions being taken as security, and often the banks acquired the use of the labour and income of an estate while a loan remained outstanding. Hence banking firms were well informed about farming conditions and often acted as agents and estate managers, with the added function of local tax collectors.

The Egibi bank of Babylon was founded as early as the seventh century BC. Not only did it float loans, receive deposits and operate a cheque system, but its capital was invested in house property, agriculture and shipping. Documents dating from 455–403 BC provide details of the flourishing commercial organisation associated with the Marashu and Sons banking house at Nippur. Accountants, assayers, loan officers and money specialists formed part of the bank's staff, and these were supported by agricultural advisers, transport specialists, irrigation experts, cattlemen and brewers. The Marashu organisation took over neglected estates and converted them into profitable enterprises. They also secured monopolies in brewing and fisheries, and extended irrigation works, selling the water to the farmers. 'Bank' is an inadequate term for such an organisation which would lend anything at a price and for a profit. Marashu even maintained its own stable of prostitutes who were rented out to understaffed brothels!

Though the private banks took over many functions initially performed by the temples and royal treasuries, both survived as financial institutions. Persepolis was the centre of a financial organisation of immense magnitude which influenced not only the life of the court but the empire as a whole. Its position was similar to that of a central or national bank, for it was able to dictate monetary policy by determining the amount of currency in circulation. At Persepolis and other royal treasuries, wealth was amassed and currency was pulled out of circulation with state hoarding. This, combined with heavy taxation, led to an acute shortage of money and interest rates soared. From 20 per cent in Babylonia before the Persian conquest they increased to 40–50 per cent by the end of the fifth century BC; in Egypt, rates were even higher. Many people, in order to pay their taxes in cash, were forced to mortgage themselves to private banks whose own shortage of cash again pushed up the price of loans.

The Persian kings were undoubtedly responsible for the empire's rapid economic advancement, but much of its serious inflationary troubles was also attributable to them. Loyalty to the empire was weakened by debt and resentment of the misuse of riches, and the hoarding of currency in the royal treasuries was another reason for the empire's ultimate decline.

# 7

# *How They Lived*

ACCURATE knowledge of the lifestyles and material cultures of the peoples of the Achaemenian empire almost exclusively concerns the kings, the royal household and the privileged classes. Such detail of everyday life comes mainly from Babylonia and it is not certain how general these conditions were throughout the empire. Babylonia, together with tax-free Persia, Ionia and Egypt, appears to have experienced a markedly higher standard of living than the provinces of the interior on the Iranian, Armenian and Anatolian plateaux. This is perhaps best illustrated in the field equipment paraded by Xerxes' expeditionary force to Greece. If body armour and metal helmets can be taken as criteria of affluence, or at least as an approximate indication of comparative wealth, then the western seaboard, Egypt, Persia and Babylonia were predominant.

In common with the majority of ancient Middle Eastern civilisations, the social structure of the Persian empire was hierarchical. This is revealed in Old Persian inscriptions, in references by the classical writers and can also be inferred from statements in the *Avesta*. The traditional unit of Iranian society had always been the patriarchal clan, with the important relationships of inheritance and succession on the male side. As social units, both the smaller family group and the larger tribe or nation were initially secondary to the clan; such a traditional system obviously applied to a predominantly nomadic existence. Though the clan continued to provide some basis for social division, particularly among the peoples of the eastern provinces, its strength was considerably modified with the development of a more settled and civilised life. Professor R. N. Frye equates the rise of the Achaemenians with the substitution of a different type of social structuring, which placed the individual in a class determined either by birth or occupation. As these divisions of society continued to evolve, the significance of the clan declined in favour of the nation on the one hand and the family group on the other.

Certainly by the time of Darius, Persian family life was a closely knit institution. Marriage was designed to secure the permanence of both family and nation; genealogies were handed down with respect and jealously guarded. All Persians longed for children and, next to prowess in war, the greatest honour was to be the father of a number of sons. Royal gifts were sent to men with large families; for the kings, judging from the number of their wives and concubines, strongly supported this 'warrior' ideal. Polygamy, and marriage between close relatives, particularly within the nobility, were blamed on foreign influence; in the same way, the Greeks were made the scapegoat for Persian homosexual and pederastic practices.

Though the *Avesta* hints at a fourfold division of society, it is not certain whether this actually existed or was merely a theory for the 'ideal' society. Some sort of class organisation must have developed under the Achaemenians, but the only concrete evidence comes from Babylonia where a multi-tier society is recognisable. At the top of this hierarchy were the king, the royal household and the courtesans. Less exalted citizens included government officials, temple priests, bankers and merchants. Brewers, butchers, carpenters and other artisans were fully fledged citizens but occupied a lower social level. All tradesmen were superior to the unskilled free labourers; at the bottom of this class structure there were the serfs and slaves.

Among the Achaemenian serfs or menials there appear to have been both domestic servants and foreign slaves. Technically the term 'slave' applied to all officers, servants and subjects of the king, but its restricted definition implied the lowest, but not necessarily the poorest, social group. Slavery in Persia was not a caste system; free men could fall into slavery, or slaves gain their freedom, whilst marriage between a free woman and a slave was by no means uncommon. Slaves consisted of prisoners of war, labourers bought in foreign markets, children sold by hard-pressed parents, and freemen whose debts or crimes had reduced them to servitude. Representing a broad cross-section of society, the slaves included many capable and intelligent men, a number of whom came to hold responsible offices, even within the royal court.

Theoretically slaves were chattels and the property of an individual, but with talent and energy one could reach a position of dignity. Servitude could be advantageous. In Babylonia, for example, many slaves lived in relative comfort on the large agricultural estates and some rented small farms, relinquishing their property rights on death. Assured of the basic requirements of food and shelter, such slaves were better off than freemen—this was one reason why children were often dedicated to serfdom by their parents.

### THE ROYAL HOUSEHOLD

The Achaemenian royal household, which formed the upper echelon of the social structure, was an extremely large institution. In addition to blood relatives of the ruling house, it included high-born Persian and Median nobles, and an assortment of foreign and local peoples who had found a place of favour at the royal court. There are numerous stories of Greeks who visited and were entertained in the Achaemenian courts, where there were Greek physicians as well as scholars, artists and architects from all over the empire. The Book of Nehemiah records how the Jew of the same name occupied for a time the position of cupbearer to Artaxerxes I. A kind of private secretary, Nehemiah had also to ensure that the king's food and drink were free from poison. Herodotus mentions the large number of foreigners who gained acceptance at the royal court. Susa, as capital of the world, was apparently thronged with princes, ambassadors, doctors, artists and men of letters.

The royal household was greatly enlarged by the harem, which was an important prerequisite of the Achaemenian rulers. This sizeable community contained not only legitimate wives and concubines but all the women in the royal household—the queen mother, sisters, cousins and others. A throng of royal offspring, including the crown prince, and a contingent of eunuchs, also lived within its closely guarded walls. Such an organised and institutionalised harem, however, appears to post-date the reign of Darius, though women exerted a strong influence in his and earlier court circles.

Though the Book of Esther is largely recognised as imagery, there is nevertheless a foundation of truth in its account of the splendours of court life and of the role and character of the harem. Following ancient traditions, women were segregated into separate buildings and the servants of the harem were emasculated before their appointment to positions of personal responsibility. When the Persians conquered the Greek islands of Lesbos and Chios, young men and girls were sent to serve in the harems. Some satrapies were forced to provide quotas of emasculated youths and maidens as part of their fixed annual tribute.

Though the harem offered little challenge during Darius' reign, in later years its political influence reached a dangerous level. Plots and intrigues rapidly increased and, under Xerxes, the harem played a dominant role in imperial affairs. Perhaps it was this that sapped the fibre of the court, reducing the latter monarchs, in the words of Icliffe, 'to a pale shadow of their great predecessors, ready to vanish before the rising sun of Alexander'.

THE CULT OF LUXURY

The conquests of Lydia, Babylonia and Egypt introduced the Persians to the riches and comforts of a civilised existence. By the time of Herodotus, their hardy, even frugal, nomadic way of life had acquired a taste for luxury which became proverbial in the ancient world. The fabulous riches of the Persians were said to be in the royal treasury at Susa—'for here,' comments Herodotus, 'where lives the Great King are the storehouses of his wealth; take that city and you need not fear to challenge Zeus for riches'. The provincial governors also touted their wealth and many of them kept smaller-scale versions of the king's court, complete with harems and treasure houses. Tritantaechmes, the satrap of Babylonia, reportedly had an income of 5 bushels of silver a day, and his own stable of 800 stallions and 16,000 mares. He had so many dogs, presumably for hunting, that four large villages received tax exemption in return for feeding the animals.

Silver and gold articles for conspicuous display and personal adornment were part and parcel of Persian aristocratic splendour. Gold earrings inlaid with enamel, brooches, armlets, roundels, winebibbers, amphorae, bowls, cups and ornamental weaponry were the products of craftsmen who blended the disparate themes of Assyria, Babylonia, Egypt and Greece with traditional Iranian motifs. This Achaemenian art-style, though hybrid, was nonetheless distinctive. One of its trademarks was a technique, derived from Egypt, of using gold and silver to produce composite items of jewellery and ornamentation. The cult of luxury was probably best demonstrated in Persian houses with their rich upholstered beds, chairs and couches; tables

The various designs on cylinder or stamp seals provide important glimpses into Achaemenian life. The subjects most favoured by the engravers were the struggle of the king with animals or monsters and scenes of the chase. The famous seal of Darius the Great (dated c500 BC) carries trilingual inscriptions and shows the king in his chariot hunting a lion. Other seals carry various motifs of religious significance including the worship of Ahura Mazda where the worshippers are represented as antithetic men symbolically supporting the winged disc of the god

Three miles (five kilometres) north of Persepolis are the royal Achaemenian tombs (sixth-fifth century BC) at Naqsh-i-Rustan. Carved into the cliffs of Kuh-i-Husain, they appear as deep crosses with their bases about 30ft (10m) above the ground. The entrances are on the central ledges whose pilasters and capitals support symbolic friezes

overlaid with gold, silver and carved ivory; carpets and tapestries; elaborate dinner services, and gold and silver cups enriched with crystal and coloured glass. A passage in Aristophanes' *Acharnians* records that an Athenian embassy, travelling in Asia Minor, was hospitably received by the Persians and given 'pure, very sweet wine' to drink in crystal and gold cups. Judging by the small fragments found in the Treasury at Persepolis, luxurious glass tableware was as much in favour with the nobility as were services in gold and silver. This opulence and the Achaemenian tradition and design were inherited by the Parthians, and caused astonishment to both Romans and Byzantines.

Whether carpets and other handicrafts traditionally associated with Persia were in general use as household furnishings and decorations is less easy to substantiate. Carpets were undoubtedly important domestic items in the tents and encampments of nomadic peoples. It is significant that the oldest surviving Persian carpet comes from the Altai region of Asiatic Russia; dating from the fourth century BC, it was preserved, deep-frozen, in the grave of a Scythian chieftain. Similar carpets were apparently exported westwards, for copies of them are painted on the walls of third century BC tombs in northern Greece, indicating their use as wall decorations as well as floor coverings. In Xenophon's time, Timasion, a general in the Greek army, owned a Persian carpet worth 1,000 drachmae. This was obviously an object of extreme value, for one drachma represented a high daily wage for a skilled labourer. Carpets must have been items of importance within Achaemenian grand houses; in the palaces they probably hung between columns and pillars, not only for decorative effect but as protection from the sun and wind and, above all, providing privacy.

Detail from the 'Darius Vase' (c325 BC) illustrating the idea of a Graeco-Iranian cultural fusion which preceded similar ideas actively encouraged by Alexander the Great. Darius III Codomanus is enthroned, surrounded by scenes depicting Greek and Persian associations

Persian wealth and luxury was also carried to the battlefields and the mess tents of officers on active duty. When Xerxes led his armies to Greece, Herodotus says that 'of all the troops the Persians were adorned with the greatest magnificence . . . they glittered all over with gold, vast quantities of which there were about their possession'. Persian generals campaigned far afield with 'furniture of gold and silver . . . gold bowls, goblets and drinking vessels'. This lavishness made a deep impression on the Greeks, especially on the frugal Spartans whose general, Pausanias, after the battle of Plataea, ordered a banquet to be prepared in the manner of both Sparta and Persia, using the royal tent and captured equipment of the Persian generals. The profusion of cups, couches and exotic foods was so magnificent that Pausanias, gathering together his generals, exclaimed: 'Men of Hellas, I called you here because I desire to show you the foolishness of the leader of the Medes, who, with such provision for life as you can see, came hither to take away from us ours that is so humble.' According to another story, when Persian ships were wrecked off Magnesia, in Greek Thessaly, a local farmer, Aminocles of Sepias, gained great wealth by collecting the gold and silver drinking vessels and countless precious objects that were washed ashore.

### DWELLINGS AND PALACES

The palaces of the kings and the grand residences of land-owners and provincial governors must have been objects of splendour and amazement to the ordinary citizens of the empire, whose lifestyles were completely divorced from the opulence of the administrative and court circles. Excavations at a settlement near the royal palace of Susa provide some information on local vernacular building styles and on general levels of comfort. The small one-room habitations were constructed in family blocks, a characteristic of both rural and urban areas. The building materials were sun-dried mud-bricks; the floors were of mud and the walls windowless. A small vestibule around the open doorway gave the inhabitants some privacy. Higher-grade dwellings consisted of a number of small rooms facing on to an inner courtyard which, in true Middle Eastern fashion, formed the social centre of the household. Both types of building were common to the Mesopotamian lowlands where stone and timber, being in short supply and expensive, were reserved for temples, palaces and the houses of the élite.

The magnificence of the Persian imperial palaces was intended to dazzle both subject peoples and foreigners. In their architecture and ornamentation, they demonstrated royal power and acted as guides to the opulence of the court. Little remains of ancient Ecbatana, though Polybius provides a graphic description of the palace. 'The woodwork was all cedar and cypress, but no part of it was left exposed, and the rafters, the compartments of the ceiling, and the columns in the porticoes and colonnades were plated with either silver or gold, and all the tiles were silver.' Pasargadae was equally ornate; the palace complex included a series of private rooms and areas exclusively used for the receptions and banquets that followed royal audiences. The surviving monuments of Pasargadae are widely scattered. It was not so much a place to walk in as to ride in. At Susa, the plan and arrangement of the palace were similar to Pasargadae, but its grandiose scale made it one of the greatest of Persian building projects. It consisted of a series of interior courts opening on to rooms and living quarters which were surrounded and linked by long corridors. Panels of beautifully coloured glazed bricks, which served the same role as tapestries, formed the most notable feature of Susa's decoration. Many of the designs executed in relief were of winged bulls, lions and the famous royal guards. The throne-room or audience-hall (*apadana*) comprised an open area whose roof was supported by six rows of six columns, nearly 66ft (20m) in height, surmounted by capitals with protomes of bulls—an architectural feat previously unparalleled. On the north, east and west sides of the throne-room there were three peristyles of twelve columns and it was approached by three wide staircases.

A long inscription, known as the 'Foundation Charter', describes the building programme for the Susa palace. Cedarwood was obtained from Lebanon, gold from Sardis and Bactria, turquoise from Chorasmia, silver and ebony from Egypt, lapis lazuli and cornelian from Sogdiana, yakawood from Kerman, ivory from Ethiopia and stone from Elam. The nationalities of the craftsmen who fashioned these materials were also recorded, thus emphasising the character of the empire as a mosaic of peoples under an all-powerful ruler, pooling their talents in a joint enterprise. 'At Susa,' Darius stated, 'a very excellent [work] was ordered; a very excellent [work] was [brought to completion].'

PERSEPOLIS

Nowhere in the empire was the magnificence of the age better expressed than in the architecture and decoration of Persepolis. The palace complex represented the culmination of Achaemenian art form, which was essentially an official court art, ceremonial in character, and designed to render to the king the homage that was due to him. Persepolis was the grandiose synthesis of all that was being built throughout the ancient world. Craftsmen and overseers, whom Darius had employed at Susa, were brought to perfect their work there. Scholars have criticised the cosmopolitan nature of Achaemenian art on the grounds that it lacked originality and was deprived of a certain freedom of expression. The gigantic structures of Persepolis, however, remained harmonious throughout; the decoration in low and high relief was powerful in its overall conception, though realism was kept within the limits of the essential. The distinctive animal-headed capitals of kneeling bulls or griffins, while fulfilling a decorative role, were essentially supports for primary and secondary beams.

The site of Persepolis was a great terrace, with its back to the mountain, partly quarried out of the rock and partly constructed of large blocks of stone. It is the pacific character of the

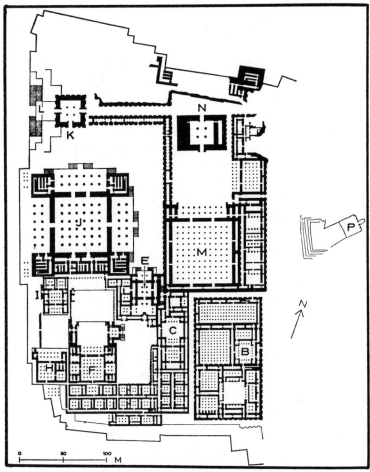

Fig 8 Plan of Persepolis: B Treasury; C Harem; E Central Hall; F Place of Xerxes; H Unidentified Palace; I Palace of Darius; J Apadana; K Gate of Xerxes; L North-western stairway; M Throne Hall of Xerxes; N Processional gateway; P Rock-cut tomb.

palace complex (Figure 8) that is most impressive; though it had some defences, it was not designed as a fortress but as a rallying centre for the nations under Persian domination. By the reign of Artaxerxes I, Persepolis had become, in the words of R. N. Frye, 'a kind of provincial Versailles'.

A monumental staircase, the sole access to the terrace, led to the gateway of Xerxes or the 'gateway of all nations'. Three impressive doors opened to the east, west and south; the east door led to the Hall of a Hundred Columns, and the south door to the king's audience hall, the *apadana*. In this replica of the throne room at Susa, the ceiling of cedarwood was supported by seventy-two fluted columns over 66ft (20m) high and surmounted by protomes of bulls and horned lions. The principal interest of the *apadana*, however, lay in the exceptional decoration of its staircases, depicting a long procession of guards, courtiers and subject peoples.

To the south of the *apadana* were the central palace, the palaces of Darius and Xerxes, and the unfinished palace attributed to Artaxerxes III. The southern windows of Xerxes' palace overlooked the extensive *anderoun*, or harem quarter (part of it has been reconstituted as a museum). Immediately to the north-west was the Hall of the Hundred Columns; apart from its height, this was of similar dimensions to the *apadana*. The nearby Treasury of Darius and the stables completed the palace complex. The function of this Hall is not known but archaeologists suggest it could have been Xerxes' throne room, an army room, or a second chamber of the treasury. It was probably here that the fatal fire was started which destroyed Persepolis in 330 BC.

### PERSIAN GARDENS

The sites of Persepolis and Pasargadae are today desolate and austere. Though experimental agricultural stations are attempting to turn Fars into a fertile province, its landscape remains largely barren. In antiquity the region appears to have been more productive, for Pasargadae was associated with a series of gardens and parks, while on the plain of Persepolis grew flowers and fruit trees. The nobility and owners of vast estates created private 'paradises'—kings and nobles used the Persian term 'paradise' to describe gardens, planned enclosures and hunting parks—in which they imagined themselves living the life of their ancestors; this was a 'back to nature' move, according to J. Lindsay. Hunting was certainly a preoccupation of the Persian nobility and is depicted on cylinder seals and other art items.

The Achaemenians also favoured the smaller, more intimate and formal retreat, which in later centuries materialised as the traditional Persian garden. There is evidence that its prototype was at Pasargadae where excavations have revealed a walled park with pools, canals and walkways. Xenophon relates how the Persian prince, Cyrus the Younger, astonished the Spartan Lysander when conducting him around his garden at Sardis, where he was governor. Cyrus informed Lysander that he had planned it all, and that when he was not on campaign he always gardened before dinner. Lysander was full of admiration for the 'beauty of the trees, the accuracy of their spacing, the straightness of their rows, the regularity of the angles and the sweet scents as they walked'. Though this was more of an orchard or smallholding than a garden, it obviously set a pattern for subsequent Persian retreats.

### FEASTS AND FESTIVALS

The greatest Persian celebration, the springtime festival of Nawruz or New Year, took place at Persepolis. Here, subservient kings, provincial governors and subject peoples in general gathered to pay homage and bring gifts to the King of Kings. A vivid picture of these sumptuous fêtes is shown in the Persepolis bas-reliefs, which have been extensively studied by archaeologists. Long before Nawruz, the grandees of the empire and delegations of the subject peoples arrived at Persepolis and pitched their tents by the thousand in the plain that stretches westwards of the palace. Foreigners were not admitted to the celebrations which partly accounts for the fact that up to the time of Alexander the Great no western writer so much as mentions Persepolis.

The New Year parade was opened by the princes of the kingdom, Persians and Medes, escorted by Susian guards and
squadrons of royal cavalry. They moved in procession up the
monumental staircase to the *apadana* and there they rendered
allegiance to the king who, with his retinue, watched from a
royal box. Then followed the procession of tribute-bearers from
all the nations bringing their gifts to the foot of the throne in
token of their fidelity and loyalty. The Susians offered weapons
and lions; the Armenians, vases of precious metals and horses;
the Babylonians, cups, embroidered textiles and oxen; the Sog-
dians, sheep and textiles; the Lydians, gold, metalwork and
horses; the Indians, weapons and mules; and the Cappado-
cians and Phrygians, horses and embroidered garments. The
king then gave a banquet and subsequently took part in a
second ceremony in which he was carried on high, seated on his
throne, by the dignitaries of the nations.

This celebration to mark the spring equinox—21 March—
was even more elaborate under the succeeding Sassanid
dynasty and has survived in Iran to this day. The New Year is
currently announced with cannons, the preparations of special
meals and the enactment of a number of ancient rites designed
to expel evil forces. The large reception given by the Shah to
his visitors must certainly be a tradition inherited from Persian antiquity.

For local or domestic celebrations the Achaemenians were
equally ready to entertain, give banquets and organise festi-
vals. This was largely attributable to their fondness for food
and wine. The sub-satrap of Judah dined at his table 150 officers daily. According to Herodotus, however, 'of all the days
in the year, the one they celebrate most is their birthday'. On
this occasion even more food than usual would be supplied
and the richer citizens would prepare a whole ox, horse, camel
and ass—whether these were alternatives or complemented
each other is not made clear. In spite of these sizeable joints,
the aristocratic Persians were much more interested in a great
variety of desserts and they drank liberally. Over-indulgence
rarely led to the Persians disgracing themselves, however. As

Herodotus explains, 'to vomit, or perform other private actions in the presence of another' was considered the highest transgression of good taste and social etiquette. 'In this,' Icliffe maintains, 'they rather resembled the French in manners than, let us say, the medieval English or Roman gastronomers.' The Persians fully appreciated the effects of strong drink and any decisions taken when they were drunk were reconsidered when they were sober. Conversely, they believed that there was some truth 'in wine' and sober decisions were frequently re-assessed in a state of inebriation.

### DRESS AND ADORNMENT

Largely on account of the detailed Persepolis reliefs and other palace decorations, more is known of the general attire of the Achaemenians and their subjects than of other aspects of their day-to-day existence. In an empire the size of ancient Persia, dress styles varied considerably, reflecting the geographical homelands of its peoples and their social and economic backgrounds. The famous tribute-bearers' frieze at Persepolis depicts twenty-three groups from various lands clad in their distinctive costumes, headgear and footwear—unfortunately no female figures are shown. In other reliefs, the male costumes are solely those of dignitaries and noblemen, and are ceremonial in character.

The Persians are invariably presented as wearing long, flowing robes—*candys*—tied at the waist with a sash or belt. This garment was formerly thought to have been fashioned from a rectangular piece of cloth with a slit in the middle through which the wearer put his head; but experiments to reproduce this dress, with its regular, though stylised, folds, have shown that it consisted of two parts, a skirt and a cape. Though apparently unsuitable for rigorous activities, it proved an adaptable costume even for hunting, when the cape was thrown back over the shoulders and the skirt was tucked into the belt. In his search for prototypes, Bernard Goldman concluded that this style was a product of the general region, similar costumes being depicted in early Luristan bronzes and in a number of pictorial representations from Hittite sites. John Boardman comments on the parallel between this albeit developed form of drapery and fashions illustrated in early sixth century Greek art.

Skirts and robes were traditional attire for males throughout the classical world. Alexander the Great, during his campaigns in Asia, refused to wear trousers—in spite of their value as riding garments, he regarded them as effeminate. Trousers formed part of the traditional dress of many peoples of western Asia, particularly the Medes whose stiff leather costumes and long cloaks further distinguished them from the Persians. Assyrian art shows the Medes wearing sheepskin coats or leopard-skin capes, with calf-length laced boots. This type of clothing, customary for men from upland areas, was accompanied by pointed caps with broad forehead bands. At Persepolis the Median hat is shown as round-topped or domed and tied on by ribbons.

The Persians, like the Babylonians, adorned themselves lavishly with jewellery and cosmetics. Gold and silver earrings, necklaces and armlets were worn by both men and women; tunics were richly embroidered and often encrusted with gems. Fluted tiaras, decorated with pearls or precious stones, completed the noblemen's sartorial elegance. It was not uncommon for ornately carved walking-sticks to be carried. Such flamboyance was equally characteristic of the army—the richly ornamented costumes depicted on the royal escort frieze at Susa being partly responsible for the declamations of Greek rhetoricians against Persian 'effeminacy'. Their liberal use of scents, ointments, face cosmetics and hair dyes must also have intrigued the Greeks. In the absence of soap, scent baths and massage were the main ways of caring for the human body; the Persians apparently liked to anoint themselves with bistre and belladona.

# 8

# What They Thought,
# Wrote and Believed

In terms of intellectual development the Achaemenian empire presents a strange dichotomy. On the one hand, the ancient Persians were mystics and individualists, concerned with the content, meaning and objectives of life. In this they were capable of developing lofty and abstract philosophical ideas, particularly in the field of monotheistic religion. Zoroastrianism (see page 122) was a factor of major importance in shaping Persian civilisation for more than 1,000 years and this religion is undoubtedly the most significant contribution of the ancient Persians to the world. In it are rooted the tolerance, flexibility, devotion to truth and other lofty principles on which the empire was based. On the other hand, it is somewhat surprising, in view of these reactionary and revolutionary ideas, to find that the Persians showed little innovation or invention in the more secular fields of intellectual progress. They revealed little interest or ability in artistic and scientific advancement, and their system of education, when compared with that of the ancient Greeks or Romans, remained rudimentary and parochial. Sporadic achievements in these fields were due chiefly to the priesthood or to individuals, generally foreigners, attached to the royal courts.

The Persians were great imitators and borrowers, and the scientific and artistic achievements of Babylonia, Greece and Egypt made up for their own lack of initiative within these fields. This cultural borrowing and adaptation is typified by Achaemenian art, especially architecture, where elements from all parts of the empire merged to produce a composite form.

The Persians were fortunate in that many of their subject peoples were well advanced in science and technology, and especially in medicine. The medical school of Demokedes, a Greek doctor from Croton in southern Italy, was famous in the ancient world, and his career was varied and profitable before he was captured in Greece and taken to Persia. Demokedes, who became physician to the royal household, treated Darius for a sprained ankle and cured Queen Atossa of an ulcer in the breast. Ctesias, whose appointment as physician to the Achaemenian crown is confirmed by Diodorus, seems to have spent much of his time in Babylon rather than in Susa and other capitals. Babylon was renowned for its advances in medicine. Potions, inhalations, suppositories, enemas, liniments, ointments and poultices were administered; wounds were cauterized with heat and sometimes taped or stitched. Absorbent lint, linen swabs and bandages were commonly used, and chemicals, such as sulphur, arsenic, mercury and antimony, were incorporated into medicines. The Babylonians also had some knowledge of the workings of the brain and the spinal cord, and the function of the heart as a pump.

The Babylonians bequeathed much more than medical science to the Persians. They had long understood mathematics and used reference tables for multiplication, division, and square and cube roots. They had mastered many theorems in geometry and solved mathematical problems with methods similar to those used in modern algebra. The Mesopotamian peoples in general had applied themselves from early times to empirical observances and measurements of cosmic phenomena. This was an attempt to formulate regular laws and to forecast future occurrences, such as eclipses. Gradually the concept of the Zodiac was attained, with the year divided into months, though initially this was not as precise as that devised by the Egyptians. The Babylonian year comprised 360 days, an extra month being added periodically to match the course of the sun and seasons. With such achievements in various fields of science the name of Babylon was held in high esteem throughout the Persian empire and ranked as its chief cultural province.

## SYSTEM OF TRAINING

It appears, from the brief outlines recorded by Herodotus, Xenophon and others, that no institutionalised or formal system of education existed among the Persians. However, boys, especially the sons of noble and prominent men, underwent a rigorous course of training which in essence was chivalrous, with great stress laid on valour, physical accomplishments and traditional attitudes. It was from such leading families that appointments were made to the army, the royal courts and provincial administration.

This training may have been partly based on the tenets of Zoroastrianism and was certainly geared to the concept of pride, an essential element in the Persian character. 'The Persians,' states Herodotus, 'regard themselves by far the best of men'—as revealed by their intense pride in both king and country.

With the emphasis on virtue, Persian youths were instructed in three things: to ride, to draw the bow and to speak the truth. These principles were obviously inherited from their nomadic ancestry and, together with plainness of diet, acted as a foil to the cult of luxury which increased with the wealth of the empire. Persian horsemanship and accuracy with the bow were legendary in the ancient world; and the love of truth was exemplified by the Persians' good faith regarding treaties and by their kings carrying out promises. Decadence and perversion, however, were criticised by Xenophon: 'where virtue once, now vice often is learnt'. This 'vice' was probably homosexuality and pederasty—'the unnatural lust' which, Herodotus states, the Persians acquired from the Greeks.

Boys were trained in a setting similar to a cadet school located at the nearest royal court or satrapal centre. Between the ages of five and fifteen they were introduced to basic martial disciplines—a training which the Greek writers comment on with admiration. Infantry and cavalry tactics were taught to groups of fifty under a nominal officer, and the competitive spirit was further encouraged in gruelling cross-country races. Boys were also trained to endure extremes of temperature and to scavenge for provisions. At the age of twenty, recruits were ready to serve in the king's army where many remained until retirement.

In addition to general military training, boys from the most prominent Persian families were prepared for their future roles as satraps, judges and royal officers, and received instruction in the practices and protocol of the royal court.

### LANGUAGE

There was a high degree of illiteracy among the nobles and even the kings. 'It was written and read to me,' reports Darius, in the Behistun inscription. In the Book of Esther, Xerxes, finding himself sleepless at night, sends for a scribe to read him some files. These scribes, drawn chiefly from Babylonia, had a tradition of conducting orderly business correspondence and cataloguing. Used extensively as secretaries by the Achaemenian kings, they were among the most important functionaries in the royal service and were expected to master and translate a variety of languages. The Book of Ezra is full of references to the efficiency of the scribes and their system of record keeping. Old Persian—one of the divisions of the Indo–European family of languages—was the vernacular speech of the Achaemenians, but royal edicts, dictated to scribes, were also written in Elamite, Akkadian and subsequently Aramaic.

Cuneiform signs, consisting of straight lines and angles impressed by a sharp-edge stylus on to clay or stone, were used to express the Persian language. Cuneiform had been gradually adopted by the Akkadians, Babylonians, Assyrians, Kassites and Elamites, who employed innumerable sign variations. The Persians reduced these to around forty, of which only four were genuine ideograms, three were signs for vowels and the rest were pure consonants, or syllables formed by consonants and vowels. Old Persian script was thus an artificial creation combining cuneiform outlines with a number of alphabetic signs drawn from Aramaic. Darius and his successors used it on their buildings, tombs and rock-carved edifices, but both linguistically and historically these inscriptions are limited in value. About 5,800 words in all, they are largely repetitious statements of kingship and religious piety, and lists of lands and peoples under Achaemenian rule. Only about 500 different words can be gleaned from the inscriptions, many of them names of people, places and months.

The repetition of words in different languages, however—especially at Behistun, where Darius' famous inscription is written in Old Persian, Akkadian (Neo-Babylonian) and Neo-Elamite—led to the initial deciphering of cuneiform writings. The identification of proper names occurring in all three versions is attributable first to the nineteenth-century work of Grotefeld, a Göttingen lecturer, and to the French scholars, Burnoff and Lassen. In 1847 the Behistun inscription was successfully copied and translated by Sir Henry Rawlinson, military adviser to the Shah. The Elamite text was translated by the English scholar, Norris, in 1853; subsequently, the Akkadian version was unravelled. In the 1950s Professor Cameron, of the Oriental Institute of the University of Chicago, descended the cliff face to make a latex impression of the inscriptions, thus ensuring complete accuracy.

Though Old Persian was the native tongue of the Achaemenian kings, it took a modest place in the government of their empire. The imperial languages of the three administrative capitals—Elamite for Susa, Old Persian for Ecbatana and Akkadian for Babylon—were on a par with each other. There were also unofficial languages and scripts in other parts of the empire, particularly in Greece and Egypt. Cyrus and his successors condoned the use of Hebrew as an everyday language. This polyglot situation proved clumsy in meeting the practical needs of imperial administration and commerce, and gradually Aramaic was adopted as the *lingua franca*.

A Semitic language with a twenty-seven-letter alphabet and a flowing script, and resembling Hebrew, Aramaic was immeasurably easier to write than cuneiform and since it could be written in ink on leather or papyrus, provided a more efficient vehicle of communication. It was the language of the Aramaeans who—in Akkadian texts of the fourteenth century BC—are spoken of as nomads of northern Arabia. They took part in the invasions of Egypt in the thirteenth and twelfth centuries and surged northwards into what is now Syria and Jordan, creating the small states of Petra, Palmyra and Edessa. By Persian times the Aramaic language was widely understood from the Mediterranean coast to Mesopotamia—hence its active promotion for commercial purposes. Its use extended far to the east, where it seems to have influenced some Indian scripts.

Cuneiform writing was not eclipsed by Aramaic, however, for Akkadian and Elamite were still used in drawing up legal documents and business contracts of a more permanent nature. It took many years of study to master cuneiform, especially Akkadian with its 600 signs, and it remained in use among the scribes for scholarly and esoteric purposes. According to Professor Cameron, in his study of the Persepolis Treasury Tablets, when an order in Old Persian was received from a high court official, a scribe translated it into Aramaic and wrote it on papyrus. A second scribe then translated the text into Elamite and inscribed it upon a tablet. Of the cuneiform scripts, Old Persian is thought to have suffered most and, by the time of the later Achaemenian kings, it had greatly declined in significance. Scholars base this view on the number of bad errors found in later inscriptions, indicating the lack of skill among scribes and their unfamiliarity with the letters and conventions of Old Persian cuneiform. The successors of Darius and Xerxes appear to have merely reproduced, with a few innovations, the texts of the earlier kings. The lack of personal stamp in such inscriptions suggests that they were drafted by scribes whose initiative rarely extended beyond copying what was already inscribed.

The use of cuneiform as a whole had disappeared by 140 BC,

except for a few priests who employed it for another half-
century; but it continued to be used for astronomical texts until
the time of Christ.

## LIBRARIES AND ARCHIVES

Though there is little evidence that the Achaemenian kings
cared much about recording their history, they did, as public
and private written documents became more com-
mon, introduce better ways for their preservation and consultation. The prototypes of libraries were undoubtedly the
Assyrian archives and collections, which included not only receipts, levy lists and official and private correspondence but
also pieces of epic poems, prayers, liturgies, mystical writings,
chronicles and astronomical calculations. These libraries were
either state institutions or privately owned by individuals or
temples. There were similar archives at Babylon, and other,
less complex institutions were founded in the Persian capitals,
the best known being at Persepolis.

Unlike the Assyrian documents, the Persepolis Treasury
Tablets contain no information of historical significance—such
as treaties, chronicles or royal edicts. They are records or letters
in Elamite, requesting payment for work completed or memo-
randa calling for reimbursement of sums paid out. Some 30,000
tablets (each measuring $1\frac{1}{2} \times 1\frac{1}{4}$in—36×30mm) and fragments of
tablets, uncovered in 1933–4 in the northern fortified wall area of
Persepolis, dated from between 514 and 510 BC. Some larger
tablets dating from 492 to 460 BC, were excavated in 1938 and
1939 in the ruins of the Treasury. Few complete tablets were
found, in proportion to the large number of fragments, and only
114 contained enough textual material to warrant translation.

## RELIGION

The impulse which drove the Persians to the conquest of the
ancient world was, according to one unfounded opinion, in

essence a spiritual enthusiasm inspired by the life and teachings of the prophet Zoroaster. Attractive as this theory is, there is no evidence that the Achaemenians used Zoroastrianism for practical politics; in fact, the reverse seems true, for freedom of religion formed part of the Persian philosophy of tolerance and flexibility. It is reasonable to suppose that at least until the reign of Darius there was no organised state religion, though this remains one of many unanswered questions concerning the Persians and their beliefs. The exact nature of Zoroaster's teachings, and where and when he taught, are also uncertain. Initially it was claimed that Zoroaster was born in the middle of the sixth century BC, but an earlier date, perhaps back to 1000 BC, is now taken as more reasonable. Many of the legends associated with Zoroaster reveal a direct parallel with the early life of Jesus Christ. He was miracuously conceived; all nature rejoiced at his birth; attempts were made by a prince to murder him; he retired into the mountainous wilderness to meditate; he was led into the presence of God and given divine revelation.

At the time of Zoroaster's mission, the traditional Iranian religion was a crude form of polytheism, similar to that of the Indians, and encompassing a host of gods and lesser deities. The chief Iranian deity, called simply Ahura or 'Lord', was akin to the Indian sky-god, Varuna. Another important deity was Mithra, who was closely associated with the sun and served as a protector of pastures, homes and treaties. The pantheon of *Daevas*, or spirits, included Mah (the moon), Vayu (wind) and Atar (fire), and it appears that all forces of nature were worshipped. Zoroastrianism was a reaction against both polytheism and the practice of blood rites, which stemmed from the traditional Aryan religion. In this connection it had much in common with Buddhism—which was almost contemporary to it. Ethnically, however, both religions derived not from the Aryan invaders but from native sources reacting against the cults and rituals of the intruders.

Although Zoroaster, or Zarathustra, may have been a native of Media, his prophesying activities took place in Choresmia (Khuvrazmish), the region of the lower Oxus, south of the Aral

Sea. As a result of his teachings he was probably expelled from Media, finding refuge in the east with Vishtaspa, who was perhaps a chief of a Choresmian confederation later overthrown by Cyrus. Zoroaster's message—the existence of two aboriginal principles: the Truth (Good, Light) and the Lie (Evil, Darkness)—is inseparable from this milieu—that of a peaceful herding population subject to the harassment of nomadic marauders. The moral dualism between the Truth and the Lie had its counterpart in the fierce opposition of herdsmen and cattle-breeders to nomadic warriors.

### THE AVESTA

The *Avesta*, the sacred book of Zoroastrianism, was written in an eastern Iranian dialect, similar to the Sanskrit of the Indian Vedas—traditionally, it was said, in gold ink on 12,000 ox-hides—only to be destroyed by Alexander the Great. Zoroaster's teachings were not in fact put into writing until long after Alexander and probably the literature that survives is only a part of the original.

The *Avesta* is divided into three parts. The *Yasna* is the main liturgy, having as its nucleus the *Gathas*, hymns and songs reputed to represent the teachings of Zoroaster. These preserve a more ancient language dating back to the tenth century BC and are similar to the Hebrew Psalms though lacking their overtones of vengeance and nationalism. The second part of the *Avesta*—*Yashts* and ancillary texts—is a series of hymns directed to various deities. The third part, *Videvdat* (law against demons), is a section on moral precepts. With the exception of the *Gathas*, the *Avesta* represents a stage of Zoroastrianism later than that preached by the prophet and reveals how his teachings were interpreted and modified with the passage of time.

AHURA MAZDA

If the *Gathas* was indeed the work of Zoroaster, the prophet is shown as a monotheist worshipping Ahura Mazda—the Wise Lord. This was a greatly exalted version of the supreme god of the ancient Iranian pantheon, and Zoroaster made him the all-powerful, all-knowing creator of the world. Zoroaster, however, was a dualist, for he assumed the existence of two aboriginal principles the Truth (Good, Light) and the Lie (Evil, Darkness)—the first represented by Ahura Mazda and the second by his opponent, Ahriman. These were the offspring, perhaps twins, of the androgynous Zurvan (Infinite Time), a god of the celestial firmament and arbiter of destiny. Out of Ahura Mazda came six abstract entities, known as the Sacred Immortals, who fought on his side: truth, good will and holy piety, chosen sovereignty, meekness (or perfect law), integrity and immortality. True to the religious dualism, Ahriman was aided by the *Daevas* (the ancient gods debased to become demons)—evil thoughts, lies, misgovernment, rebellion, infirmity and death. Between the two stood man, endowed with moral freedom on which depended his fate beyond the grave.

  Zoroaster claimed to have a special revelation from Ahura Mazda, and from this he created a religious, philosophical and ethical system designed to bring man and the world to salvation. A series of prohibitions were placed on all actions through which the spirit of evil might gain victory, and there were injunctions to do good works and thus conquer the allies of Ahriman. The new cult brought a reduction in ancient Indo-Aryan ceremonies and rituals, especially blood sacrifice and the use of stimulating drink (*haoma*). The old Aryan religions according to Professor Frye, were 'rite-centred', whereas the reforms of Zoroaster were 'belief-centred'. The message of Zoroaster was lofty and abstract for, against the current pagan polytheism, he set a universal system of metaphysical ideas—a religion, in the modern sense. The belief proclaimed by Zoroaster was trust in the goodness and justice of Ahura Mazda, and faith that in the end only he would be victorious, even when smaller battles were won by Ahriman. Many scholars maintain that the Book of Job is a Judaised Zoroastrian story to illustrate the unreplenished power of truth overcoming the replenished power of evil. In man's struggle for truth, Zoroaster promised prosperity in this world and immortality hereafter. He also believed that the end of the world would come in due season, at which time Ahura Mazda would signify his triumph by sending a purifying freshet of molten metal to engulf the wicked.

THE MAGI

The Magi—the Zoroastrian priesthood—were probably a hereditary caste entrusted with the supervision of religion through a formal ritualistic system which included rules of purification. According to Herodotus, 'without a Magus it is not lawful for them [the Persians] to offer sacrifice'; in this role the Magi were comparable with the Brahman caste of the Hindus. The Magi, natives of Media, appear to have held a monopoly on religious practices and, hence, considerable power throughout the western part of the Achaemenian empire. They had probably been the priests of polytheistic communities and had played a leading role in the civil wars following the death of Cambyses. Gaumata had been a Magi, and Darius, on his succession, ordered the slaughter of priests—an event that was celebrated annually. Ultimately the Magi were allowed back in court, where they were important members, at least from the reign of Xerxes onwards.

The Magi were technical experts on all forms of worship rather than representatives of one particular religion. Zoroastrianism, in its purest form, was too abstract to persist unchanged and in the hands of the Magi its lofty principles degenerated into formal observances. Almost immediately, elements of the old polytheism reappeared and the Magi came to regard Ahura Mazda within the pantheon of non-Zoroastrian deities, an approximate equivalent of the Greek

Zeus. His attributes became personified as separate gods; together with Ahura Mazda, they comprised a heptad known as the Bounteous Immortals. His closest allies were Mithra, the sun god, and Anahita, the spirit of fertility.

RITES AND RITUALS

The upgrading of Mithra and Anahita transformed the purity of Zoroastrianism into Mazdaism, in which fire-worship and its purification rites were strongly emphasised. Fire was the purest manifestation of Ahura Mazda. On the carved reliefs of the Achaemenian tombs, fire altars are depicted, and above them hovers the figure of the god. Mazdaism was subsequently developed into Mithraism, especially under the successors of Alexander the Great (see Chapter 9).

Religious ritual was further complicated by the reintroduction and consecration of the *haoma* rites which had played an important role in the older Iranian cults. According to the *Avesta*, *haoma* was the name of a plant; the extract obtained from pounding its twigs, states Jacques Duchesne, was the alkaloid ephedrine, which in rituals was probably mixed with milk to disguise its taste. The Persepolis Treasury Tablets name priests whose duty it was to prepare *haoma*, and a number of mortars and pestles have been discovered which were probably used for this purpose. Another outlawed rite that returned under the guise of Zoroastrianism was the sacrifice of animals, though now they were stunned before being killed with a knife.

Regulations in the *Avesta* prohibited the building of temples or statues to Ahura Mazda. The concept of the supreme god, perfect in all things, was too vast to allow any shelter for him except the vault of heaven. Herodotus comments on this: 'The custom of the Persians is not to raise statues, temples and altars to the gods; on the contrary they treat those who do as madmen; in my opinion, this is because they do not believe like the Greeks that the gods have a human form.' Yet Ahura Mazda is often represented on Achaemenian monuments as a bearded man, crowned with a tiara and enclosed in a winged solar disc; the bust is of a modified Assyrian type and the disc in the Egyptian style. This transgression of the precepts of the *Avesta* was brought about by the progress in art and the Achaemenian tolerance which only penetrated into the monumental sculpture of palaces and tombs.

Both cremation and burial of the dead were prohibited, so as to avoid contamination of earth or fire. Nor could corpses be thrown into rivers, for this polluted water. Bodies were exposed in 'towers of silence' until their flesh had rotted or been consumed by birds. These Achaemenian funeral rites, which greatly intrigued Herodotus, created a type of architecture unknown outside Iran. The towers were tall, built of unadorned masonry, and supported a wooden trellis-work on which the corpses were laid. According to Herodotus, the skeletons were later covered in wax, to avoid all direct contact with the ground, and then placed in nearby ossuaries.

These towers were used only for common burials. The kings transgressed the 'law' and were buried in tombs. Cyrus' mausoleum at Pasargadae is unique; it consists of a single chamber with a gabled roof, standing on a platform approached by six steps. The burial chamber, which in effect is a large sarcophagus, was sealed—before its desecration—by a stone door. At Persepolis and Naqsh-i-Rustan, the later Achaemenian kings had their tombs excavated into rock faces. Externally they present a cruciform shape composed of decorative panels; probably originating in native tradition. At Naqsh-i-Rustan the entrances to the tombs of Darius I, Xerxes, Artaxerxes I and Darius II are some 70ft (20m) above the ground. The presence of two fire altars hint at some of the ceremonies that occurred here.

### THE RELIGION OF THE KINGS

It is debatable whether Zoroastrianism became the faith of peoples who were not Persian. Even among the Persians themselves only a limited circle of aristocrats and courtiers followed its doctrines fully. Whether Darius was a Zoroastrian is a much-disputed argument clouded by the difficulties of distinguishing the 'primitive' religion preached by the prophet from its subsequent adulteration at the hands of the Magi. Though a number of scholars consider Darius to have been a monotheist, he never mentions the prophet's name and his references to Ahura Mazda might have been for political purposes only. In the same vein, however, his references to other gods have been taken to reflect not a polytheistic attitude but a tolerance of gods other than his own.

After the reign of Xerxes, inscriptions left by the Achaemenian monarchs refer to deities and concepts that were incompatible with Zoroastrianism and probably reflect the change back to polytheism from monotheism. Artaxerxes II proclaims himself as worshipping Ahura Mazda, Mithra and Anahita, and Artaxerxes III invokes both Ahura Mazda and Mithra. Hence, it does not appear that strict Zoroastrianism prevailed for long, even in the Persian court. Yet the political power of the Persians ensured that the religion became at least vaguely known to the majority of peoples over whom they ruled. Subsequently in Persian history it developed as a more prominent political and cultural force.

# 9

# The Decline and the Legacy

THE foundations of Achaemenian greatness contained the seeds of its own decadence and ultimate decline. The reasons are as complex as the empire itself. Many would argue that decline was the direct result of Achaemenian tolerance and moderation, for though the idea of knitting together the empire's diverse nationalities was revolutionary, the levelling of culture in terms of a unified language, religion, or common interest, failed to materialise and this hastened its downfall. In many ways cultural diversity reflected the absence of a coherent middle class—professional, technical and artistic. Thus Achaemenian Persia was created by a few men of genius, who could conquer and govern but who were unable to provide the moral framework, the intellectual cement, or even the verbal formula, to hold a great empire together.

There were, of course, numerous contributory forces which collectively led to Achaemenian decline. The size of the empire, physically disjointed with its isolating factors of deserts and mountain ranges, made control difficult and aided regionalism. Though communications were improved and, for strategic purposes, Iranians were settled throughout the empire, rulers and ruled were too disproportionate in numbers for this policy to have lasting effect. Constant revolts in outlying provinces and the long struggle with Greece combined to foster degeneration. Nor was the central government's financial policy free from blame. The tendency to hoard precious metals withdrew too much from circulation, damaging both the national economy and international commerce; whilst the use of gold as a means of diplomacy was an easy, but dangerous, way of maintaining the empire's power and influence. Not least, there were the intrigues and rivalries within the royal household, leading to assassinations which regularly endangered the succession. On the death of Arses, the son of Artaxerxes III, so much royal blood had been shed that the only survivor to continue the Achaemenian line was a distant cousin who became Darius III.

The Achaemenian empire was dangerously unstable in the hands of lesser rulers who lacked the forceful character and energy of its founders, for so much depended on the personality of the king. The reign of Darius I is regarded as the culmination both of the power of the empire and of the whole Achaemenian culture, though for a century and a half after his death in 486 BC Persia survived, almost exclusively, on what had been fashioned and built before. This was arrested development rather than progress for Darius' successors possessed neither his generalship nor political skills and the toleration which was formerly displayed was replaced by conformity, often brutally enforced.

Xerxes, a man of few military ideas, repeated his father's mistake in an assault on the Greek city states. His inventiveness, it appears, was confined to domestic adventures, but these too, in their failure, paralleled his military exploits. Both Herodotus and the Book of Esther relate how he was prepared to sacrifice the peace of the empire to the aim of seducing the wife and daughter of a loyal brother whom he murdered. In retribution Xerxes himself died by the hand of his chief minister.

THE LATER KINGS

The rise to power through intrigue and assassination came to be the established pattern among the later Achaemenian kings. The accession of Artaxerxes I Longimanus (466–426 BC) was marked by the rebellion of his brother, the satrap of Bactria. The revolt was quickly suppressed, but to safeguard his own position Artaxerxes murdered all his brothers and married his sister. On the political and cultural front, there was an extension of relations with Greece. The Greeks aided Artaxerxes to suppress a revolt in Egypt, which was returned to the empire in 455 BC. In Babylonia, Artaxerxes followed the policies of his predecessors, but heavy taxation and the active settlement of Persians on Babylonian lands led to much unrest.

Signs of Persian decay were beginning to show, for Artaxerxes was forced to relinquish the Greek cities of Ionia and there were further territorial losses on the eastern frontiers. The Greeks no longer looked on the empire as a redoubtable enemy. Euripides, mirroring the opinions of his age, declared that 'Asia serves as a slave of Europe.' Considerable cultural exchange continued between the two worlds, however, and artists, scientist, and writers, including Herodotus, travelled throughout Greece, Iran, Babylonia and Egypt. During the reign of Artaxerxes, Persepolis ceased to be the official royal Achaemenian residence.

The death of Artaxerxes I in 426 BC was followed by civil war. Intrigue and corruption, together with the murder of two royal princes, put Darius II on the throne (425–405 BC). This accession of Artaxerxes' son by a Babylonian concubine brought to an end the true Achaemenian line. Darius was greatly influenced by his wife and half-sister, Parysatis, who favoured her younger son, Cyrus, rather than the rightful heir, Artaxerxes II. Cyrus was given extensive satrapal powers in Asia Minor, as well as command of the imperial troops, obviously, to guarantee his succession by force. The reign of Darius II was disrupted by numerous satrapal rebellions, but the Greeks, engaged in the Peloponnesian War, were unable to profit from this Achaemenian weakness. Persian gold, in fact, kept the Greek warring factions in supplies. The constant feuds within the royal household reflected Darius' tortuous foreign policies.

At the coronation of Artaxerxes II at Pasargadae in 405 BC, his brother Cyrus made a dramatic attempt on his life. After an appeal by Parysatis, Cyrus was pardoned and allowed to return to Asia Minor, where the troops were again at his disposal.

Xenophon, in *Anabasis,* describes Cyrus' second attempt to secure the Achaemenian throne, but he was killed in battle near Babylon. All the records pay tribute to Cyrus' outstanding courage. 'If he had won the throne,' states Ghirsham, 'he might perhaps have arrested the decline of the dynasty.' As it happened, Egypt regained its independence.

On his accession in 359 BC, Artaxerxes III found it expedient to engineer the murder of several dozen brothers and sisters. Though he was brutal and ruthless, his goal was to win back the empire and re-establish its former unity. With the reconquest of Egypt, the Achaemenian empire appeared stronger than at any time since Darius I. 'History might have been different,' states Frye, 'if Artaxerxes had not been poisoned at about the same time that Philip was uniting the Greeks behind him by conquering them at the battle of Chaeronea.' This materialisation of a united Greece dealt the death blow to the Achaemenian empire. Persian troops had earlier proved no match for the Greek armies, whose military qualities were abetted by the even more warlike Macedonians.

The assassination of Artaxerxes III in 338 BC was the calculated plot of Bogoas, his chief minister, who also poisoned the royal princes, with the exception of Arses. After ruling as a puppet king for a few years, Arses and his heirs also fell victim to Bogoas' exterminating policies. The sole remaining heir to the Achaemenian dynasty was a distant cousin, who took the now traditional name of Darius and became known as Codomanus. As the last Achaemenian king, Darius III was a courageous leader and established his rule by promptly poisoning Bogoas. But he was overconfident as to the might of his army and underestimated the strength of Alexander the Great. The conquest of the Achaemenian empire was to Alexander a crusade to be accomplished in the shortest possible time.

ALEXANDER THE GREAT

The Achaemenians were conquered by the Macedonians—a people with whom they had a number of features in common.

Like the Persian heartland, Macedonia was an agricultural country whose population was initially divided into tribes and clans under the authority of large land-holding chiefs. Below them lived a free peasantry and over all stood the king, exercising religious, judicial and military power. Philip of Macedon, rather like Darius I, had reorganised his kingdom, bound its people to the throne and established a formidable fighting force. The Macedonian empire was inherited by his son, Alexander (356–323 BC), whose pan-Hellenic ideals were tempered with the desire for territorial conquests and commercial interests, and the acquisition of loot and glory.

In his advance against Persia, Alexander swiftly conquered Asia Minor, occupied the Phoenician cities, invaded Egypt and moved into Mesopotamia. The decisive battles between Macedonia and Persia took place at the Granicus river crossing, the Cicilian Gates at Issus and at Gaugamela, near Arbela. At Issus and Gaugamela, Darius III fled the battlefield and took refuge at Ecbatana before escaping to the northern provinces. He was subsequently betrayed, imprisoned, and stabbed to death near Damghan by Bessus, the satrap of Bactria.

When Alexander the Great succeeded Darius, the Achaemenian capitals of Ecbatana, Susa and Babylon opened their gates to him as they had done centuries earlier to the Persian conquerors. But Persepolis was burned and looted, and it is alleged that Alexander treated its inhabitants with the utmost brutality, although it was not his policy to destroy cities or to massacre the vanquished. Of the many reasons put forward for this uncharacteristic treatment of Persepolis, that of political revenge appears the least convincing for this would more likely have been exacted at Susa, the effective capital of the Achaemenian world.

Though the destruction of Persepolis symbolically marked the end of the Achaemenian empire, its political and cultural heritage remained part of the life of the Middle East. Alexander was in effect the last of the Achaemenians, for he attempted to foster the fusion of Hellenes and Iranians, an ideal whose basis existed long before his conquest. Alexander's marriage to

Roxane, daughter of a Sogdian chief, and the mass marriage of his troops to Iranian women at Susa, were practical steps towards this union of two peoples.

In the organisation of his empire, Alexander was greatly influenced by Persian ideals and Achaemenian administrative methods, and other institutions,—although increasingly Hellenised—were preserved under the Seleucid Greek rule that followed his death in 323 BC.

### AFTER ALEXANDER

The Seleucids held Iran for only a short period. Soon after 250 BC, the Parthians, a nomadic people of Aryan origin, established themselves in north-eastern Persia under Mithradates I. Within a century the Parthians had gained control of the whole of Iran and parts of Mesopotamia, their monarchs claiming to be the restorers of the Achaemenian empire and assuming the title 'Great King'. The Parthians, being militarily strong, repeatedly resisted the advances of Rome to which they imparted the concept of empire on a grand scale.

Iranian patriotism, partly revived under the Parthians, was fully realised by the Sassanians, initially a local group from Parsa who strongly identified themselves with the Achaemenian empire. The revolt of the Sassanians against Parthian rule led to the establishment of a new dynasty in AD 224 under the leadership of Ardashir. They claimed their divine right to rule from Ahura Mazda and Zoroastrianism became the state religion.

The Sassanians were major rivals of the Romans and, subsequently, the Byzantines. Weakened by internal conflicts and attacks from the Huns and Turks, their empire fell in AD 642 to the Arabs, who had emerged as a major force in the Middle East. Yet the traditional influence of Iran was able to absorb or re-shape not only the culture of the Arabs but, later, that of the Turks and Mongols. A distinctive Persian character was thus maintained and this evolved as a decisive influence in the new cultural empire of Islam which in turn came to dominate the Middle East.

## THE ACHAEMENIAN HERITAGE

The impact any major civilisation has on the world at large is at once obvious yet subtly hidden. The famous archaeological ruins and the constantly increasing number of excavated sites are visible and concrete testaments to the character and integrity of the ancient Persian empire. Ruins, such as Persepolis, Naqsh-i-Rustan, Pasargadae and Behistun are among Iran's major tourist attractions, and the tomb of Cyrus the Great its most celebrated monument. In addition, a comprehensive coverage of Persia's early history is housed in the archaeological museum at Tehran, where major Achaemenian exhibits include monumental sculpture and reliefs, stairs, columns and enamel panels, weapons, and gold and silver ornaments. Many Persian art treasures have also found their way into museums and private collections throughout the world.

The direct contribution of Achaemenian Persia to the life of the western world may appear slight in comparison with the ideas and continuity of traditions stemming from Greece, Rome and Israel. However, the Persians played their part in many fields and particularly influenced developments in government, religion, philosophy and even language. Although the Achaemenians did not succeed in creating a universal language, many words and phrases currently employed in English and other European tongues can be traced to Old Persian origins or at least to Aramaic versions of Old Persian forms. Behind the word *magic*, for example, lies the Old Persian *magus*, a member of a priestly caste, familiar from the Magi, or the three wise men. The word *paradise*—a nobleman's hunting and pleasure park—can be traced to ancient Persia, as can the names and origins of many fruits and vegetables which probably grew there or in early Persian gardens—*lemons, oranges, melons, peaches, spinach* and *asparagus. Bazaar* is also of Iranian origin, as are the names of many of the commodities sold there—*trousers, belt, taffeta, tiara, shawl, sash, awning* and *turquoise*. Perhaps the most interesting of the Old Persian loan-words are the ones relating to those areas of greatest Achaemenian influence—government, administration and general control; in translation, and particularly common in the Old Testament, these include *counsellor, chief minister, police chief, message, corporal punishment* and *written order.*

Though Achaemenian government became the model for later empires, Iran was also the home of a number of major religious traditions. As a result of its geographical position between east and west, and with its tolerance and respect for the views of others, the empire became a great assimilator of religious beliefs and profoundly influenced subsequent western religions. Zoroastrianism, which outlasted the Achaemenian kings to become the official creed of the Sassanians, still has its followers today—about 10,000 of them in modern Iran. There are around 100,000 in India, chiefly in and around Bombay. Many are prosperous businessmen and community leaders, known as Parsees, because of their Persian origin, who fled eastwards to escape Islamic rule. Converts are not accepted; and they are not permitted to marry outside their faith. The celebration of New Year, the maintenance of the perpetual flame, the investiture of neophytes, and the use of the sacred *haoma* are all continuations of ancient and traditional rites.

Zoroastrian ideas also found their way into the religious cults of the ancient Israelites, probably at the time of the Jewish exile in Babylon. The Persians had developed the Semitic concept of an afterlife into a belief in immortality; this, together with the idea of reward and punishment, penetrated Jewish doctrines—as expressed in the Book of Daniel. The Jewish sect which gave strongest support to these beliefs were the Pharisees—a name that may derive from 'Persians'.

Zoroastrianism may also have given Judaism the concept of the devil, a powerful figure counterposed to God. Before the Babylonian exile, biblical scriptures treat Satan as an agent of God who obeyed his master's wishes, but subsequently his powers appear more reminiscent of those of Ahriman. There is a consensus of opinion that the Dead Sea Scrolls, discovered in 1947, reflect Zoroastrianism's influence on Judaism. For the Jews, however, faith and politics were fused into an indissoluble unity, whereas in Persia they were distinct.

It was natural that, through Judaism, Zoroastrianism should have a major influence on Christianity, as is reflected in Christian belief in one God, in distinguishing right from wrong and in life after death. Yet Christianity had its most potent rival in an off-shoot of Zoroastrianism—Mithraism; this became a popular religious cult throughout the Mediterranean world, particularly in Roman times. Mithra, the god of truth and light, was one of the more important pre-Zoroastrian deities; sixty Mithra temples are known to have existed in Rome. The religion was practised in most parts of the empire, including Britain. Some of the rites were analogous to those of Christian baptism, confirmation and the Eucharist. Sunday was observed as a holy day, and 25 December as the festival of the rebirth of Mithra, who took the form of mediator between the supreme deity and man.

Yet another religion was to spring from the Persians. Under the Sassanian king Shapur I, a Persian noble called Mani claimed—like Zoroaster, the Buddha and Jesus Christ—to have been sent by God. He preached a religion which combined Jewish, Christian and Buddhist elements with Zoroastrian ideas. Manichaeism, which initially found favour, was subsequently outlawed, following the execution of its leader by the Magi around AD 273, and eventually took refuge in Central Asia. To Christians, Manichaeism appeared as a Pauline heresy but its syncretic character illustrates, perhaps best of all, the role of Persia as a cultural assimilator.

On the non-spiritual level, the chief legacy of the ancient Persians to the western world must be their organisational ideals based on the concepts of unity and cohesion, combined with the largest possible freedom for the development of race and individual within the larger organism. If, in positive terms, the Persians failed to sustain this goal, they nonetheless created a tradition which was exploited and given new vigour by subsequent empires. As far as their own country was concerned, the Persians, in the face of Arab, Turk and Mongol invasions, continued to act as adapters and assimilators of influences from both east and west, at the same time preserving their essentially Iranian characteristics.

Perhaps the greatest legacy of the ancient Persians is modern Iran itself, whose revival this century has taken the form of a national renaissance. In adopting the outward forms of western civilisation, the country has remained, in spirit, faithful to its ancient traditions. 'The Persians,' says T. R. Glover, 'break upon the West with a series of surprises,' and the development, today, of a highly centralised state with a rapidly expanding economy is as significant for the West as was the rise to power of the Achaemenian kings of antiquity.

# Appendix I

CHRONOLOGY OF MAJOR ACHAEMENIAN EVENTS
(unless otherwise stated, all dates are BC)

| | |
|---|---|
| c 700 | Hakhamanish or Achaemenes founds the dynastic line |
| 675 – 640 | Reign of Teipses |
| 640 – 600 | Reign of Cyrus I, King of Anshan |
| 640 – 590 | Reign of Ariaramnes, King of Parsa |
| 600 – 559 | Reign of Cambyses I |
| 559 – 529 | Reign of Cyrus the Great |
| 547 | Battle of Pterya and incorporation of Lydia |
| 540 | Fall of Babylon |
| 538 | Trial of Grimilli |
| 529 – 522 | Reign of Cambyses II |
| 525 | Cambyses' conquest of Egypt |
| 522 | Insurrections in the Satrapies |
| 522 – 486 | Reign of Darius the Great |
| c 521 | Susa made the administrative capital |
| 512 | Expedition to Macedonia and Thrace |
| c 500 | Opening of Suez Canal |
| 499 | Rebellion of Greek Cities of Ionia |
| 490 | Battle of Marathon |
| 486 – 466 | Reign of Xerxes I |
| 480 | Battle of Salamis |
| 479 | Battle of Plataea |
| c 478 | Voyage of Sataspes |
| 466 – 426 | Reign of Artaxerxes I Longimanus |
| 455 | Egypt returned to the empire |
| 425 – 405 | Reign of Darius II |
| 405 – 359 | Reign of Artaxerxes II |
| 405 | Revolt of Cyrus III (The Younger) |
| 359 – 338 | Reign of Artaxerxes III |

# *Appendix II*

MAIN BRITISH ARCHAEOLOGICAL SITES

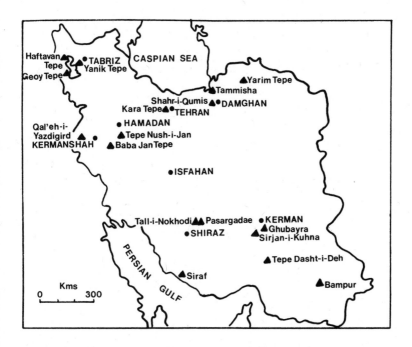

# Bibliography

ARBERRY, A.J. (ed). *The Legacy of Persia* (Oxford University Press, 1953)

BURN, A.R. *Persia and the Greeks* (Edward Arnold, 1962)

COLLINS, R. *The Medes and the Persians* (Cassell, 1974)

CULICAN, W. *The Medes and the Persians* (Thames and Hudson, 1965)

DUCHESNE-GUILLEMAN, J. *Western Response to Zoroaster* (Oxford University Press, 1958)

FINLEY, M.I. *The Greek Historians* (Chatto and Windus, 1959)

FRYE, R.N. *The Heritage of Persia* (Weidenfeld and Nicolson, 1962)

GHIRSHMAN, R. *Iran* (Penguin Books, 1954)

——*The Arts of Mankind: Persia from the Origins to Alexander the Great* trans. S. Gilbert and J. Emmons (Thames and Hudson, 1964)

HICKS, J. *The Emergence of Man: The Persians* (Time-Life Books, 1975)

HIGNETT, C. *Xerxes' Invasion of Greece* (Oxford University Press, 1963)

MATHESON, S.A. *Persia: An Archaeological Guide* (Faber and Faber, 1972)

MOOREY, P.R.S. *Ancient Iran* (Oxford University Press, 1975)

MYRES, J.L. *Herodotus, Father of History* (Oxford University Press, 1953)

OLMSTEAD, A.T. *History of the Persian Empire* (University of Chicago Press, 1960)

RICE, T. TALBOT. *The Scythians* (Thames and Hudson, 1957)
SCHMIDT. E.F. *Persepolis* (University of Chicago Press, 1957)
SELINCOURT, A. DE *The World of Herodotus* (Secker and Warburg, 1962)
——*Herodotus: The Histories* (Penguin Books, 1971)
WHEELER, M. *Flames over Persepolis* (Weidenfeld and Nicolson, 1968)
WILBER, D.N. *Persepolis* (Cassell, 1969)
ZAEHNER, R.C. *The Dawn and Twilight of Zoroastrianism* (Weidenfeld and Nicolson, 1961)

Current archaeological research in Iran is regularly reported in *Iran*, Journal of the British Institute of Persian Studies in Tehran. Appendix II indicates the main British archaeological sites.

# Acknowledgements

THE task of writing this book has been made very much easier by the help and kindness I have received from a number of individuals and organisations. The preceding pages do not pretend to original scholarship; they have been compiled almost exclusively from secondary sources, although this in itself has been an exhausting enough task. I am indebted in particular to the information supplied to me by the Tehran Archaeological Museum, the British Museum, the Oriental Institute of the University of Chicago and the Ashmolean Museum. I am also grateful to all the authors and researchers, ancient and modern, who have written on Achaemenian Persia and covered many aspects of the field before me.

On the practical side I should like to thank Mrs L. MacIver who drew the maps and diagrams and Mr B.J. Reeves for his help with the photographic illustrations. At various points the manuscript was typed by Miss A.L. Laing, Mrs J.C. Simpson and Mrs M. McLeod, and I am grateful to them for their candid opinions of its contents.

Brian Dicks, 1978

# Index